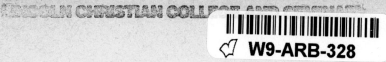

SECRETS FOR GROWING CHURCHES

Secrets for
Growing Churches

CHARLES MYLANDER

1817

Published in San Francisco by Harper & Row, Publishers

NEW YORK, HAGERSTOWN, SAN FRANCISCO, LONDON

FIRST EDITION

Designed by Jim Mennick

Library of Congress Cataloging in Publication Data

Mylander, Charles.
    SECRETS FOR GROWING CHURCHES.

    Includes index.
    1. Church growth. I. Title.
BV652.25.M93 1979   254'.5   79-1764
ISBN 0-06-066055-4

---

79 80 81 82 83   10 9 8 7 6 5 4 3 2 1

Contents

To my wife, Nancy,
perpetual delight

Preface

The purpose of this book is to help church leaders stimulate growth in their congregations. Rather than presenting one method or program, I explain practical principles that are working in growing churches. Each chapter presents a growth-stimulating "secret," with its various ramifications. The principles overlap and interact, so that for maximum growth all the secrets must operate simultaneously. The purpose is not to diagnose all the problems of nongrowing churches and to prescribe cures. This is not a medical book for sick churches (although such a work is sorely needed). The emphasis here is on what God is blessing for the growth of his churches. The principles I outline here apply across denominational and state lines. Others across the country have put them to work with success.

I entered church-growth thinking through the back door of failure. It all began a dozen years ago in a little Oregon church. For four years I put all my energy into the pastoral ministry. I logged a thousand calls a year, studied with an open mind, and gave myself without reservation to pastoral life. In spite of the hard work, long hours, much prayer, and my best efforts, the church did not grow. Morale became a problem and my role as pastor was criticized. I deeply desired some kind of breakthrough. Nongrowth meant something was wrong, but I did not know what.

In the meantime I was learning valuable lessons about faithfulness and obedience as the true measures of success. I now see how the Lord was building character and sensitivity into my life. As I matured in the ministry, the Lord helped me hold fast the basic conviction that growth is a sign of health. Hurting over our nongrowth, I began to read books by Donald A. McGavran and his associates about church expansion in various countries. Then came the breakthrough. In a church-growth seminar Medford Jones, now president of Pacific Christian College in Fullerton, California, shared simple principles about space, staff, and program. His suggestions were worth a try. I returned and made a couple of changes, and our church began to grow.

Soon thereafter my wife, Nancy, and I accepted the call to serve as minister of Christian education at East Whittier Friends Church in Whittier, California. For several years the attendance at East Whittier Friends had been slipping downward. The senior pastor, T. Eugene Coffin, and his wife, Jean, arrived six weeks after we did, and from the first showed great confidence and ability. A fresh spurt of growth became immediately evident. For five years we worked with a leader who expected growth and knew how to stimulate it. Our first baby had just arrived, and so Nancy had her hands full with Kirk, our new son. My time was divided between church and classes at Fuller Theological Seminary in Pasadena, California.

At seminary I took numerous electives from the now-famous School of World Mission. Men like McGavran, C. Peter Wagner, Ralph Winter, Arthur Glasser, and J. Edwin Orr stimulated my mind and heart. In the

School of Theology I obtained a wealth of theological background under top-notch evangelical scholars. Former pastors such as James Daane, Robert Schaper, and Robert Munger supplied practical information. The combination of intense study in church growth and practical experience under a growth-producing pastor provided a wealth of insights. My mind was spinning, my heart was burning, and my fingers were itching to write. With C. Peter Wagner and James Daane as mentors, I began research for a doctor of ministry thesis.

About this time our family, including our new daughter, Lisa, accepted the call to serve as associate pastor at Rose Drive Friends Church in Yorba Linda, California. Under the leadership of the founding pastor, C. W. Perry, this church had been growing since its beginning in 1963. Other churches showed more phenomenal explosions in membership, but the steady growth here was exciting to all involved. Approximately each five years the average attendance had doubled. With the growth came the need for additional pastoral staff, and thus the invitation for us to serve. We sensed the Lord's clear leading to accept the call and have felt confirmed in it ever since.

Rose Drive Friends Church continued to grow, and invitations to talk about it were not uncommon. Having completed my doctoral thesis and graduated, I now felt able to accept speaking engagements. Under Win Arn and the Institute for American Church Growth, both C. W. Perry and I became regular speakers at the Advanced Institute for Professionals. Other pastors' conferences from a variety of denominations and geographical areas widened our perspective and tested our practical applications. Our presentations most often met with a ready and appreciative response. Some churches put the concepts to work with remarkable results. The input of numerous church leaders stimulated my thinking and expanded the presentations into five basic lectures.

Then in April 1976, at a Friends Pastors' Conference in Dallas, Texas, D. Elton Trueblood suggested that I transform my somewhat technical thesis into a clear-thinking book for a general audience. He graciously offered to take me on as a writing student; so our correspondence began. He read the draft of each chapter and offered insights and suggestions. Then I rewrote. In the process, this book emerged.

I wish to give special credit to my lovely wife, Nancy, who shared with me in the preparation process. Her help has been beyond measure in the long and challenging task of graduate study, sorting out convictions, and learning by trial and error. Her patience and love have surpassed the requirements of duty and entered the realm of sacrifice. Norman Rohrer read each chapter and offered helpful suggestions. His writing expertise and personal encouragement helped so much. Sandi Perry typed and retyped each chapter with a warm smile, a reassuring comment, and a servant's heart. To each of these people, and to the multitude of Christian leaders who influenced my thinking, I say a heartfelt thank you!

CHARLES MYLANDER

Yorba Linda, California
Easter 1979

1. Build Your Church Morale

"Advance or Decadence are the only choices offered to mankind."
—ALFRED NORTH WHITEHEAD

An apple seed lies dormant for years, but surround it with warm soil and the right amount of moisture, and it sprouts. When the conditions are right, God causes the seed to germinate and push a tender stem toward the sunlight. Mortals cannot manufacture seeds or cause growth, but we can cooperate with the principles God built into his creation. Likewise, only God can cause the growth of a church. His coworkers, however, if they desire maximum fruit, can learn to cooperate with his purposes and principles. Apple orchards grow as a result of planned efforts by a worker who cooperates with God's natural laws. Similarly, vigorous church growth most often follows the hard work and careful planning of God's colaborers (see 1 Corinthians 3:7–9). The effectiveness of those who plant and water, the human leadership, immensely influences the yield.

A primary responsibility of church leaders is to develop an atmosphere conducive to healthy growth. A positive spirit in a church is a climate in which people flourish, and high morale is essential for a growing church. The effect is cyclical: high morale is conducive to church growth, which results in higher morale, which encourages greater growth, and so on. It happens time after time. The opposite is also true. Low morale stifles growth, which in turn hurts the morale.

ALTERNATIVES: GROWTH OR DECLINE

A local church never remains static. Two processes, perishing and growing, always operate simultaneously. A local church is constantly perishing as members slip out the back door; some move away, others become inactive. Death claims still others. At the same time, the congregation is growing as new members enter through the front door. Children take on the responsibilities of adult membership, active Christians transfer in from other congregations, nominal believers renew their relationship with the Lord and his church. Best of all, some people with no conscious commitment to Jesus Christ turn from their sinful ways and accept him as Lord and Savior.

God's colaborers must expend a tremendous amount of energy just to maintain the present size and strength of a local church. Obviously, the growing portion of the congregation must equal its perishing parts in order to maintain itself. For steady expansion, the number of new people flowing through the front door must exceed the number of those quietly leaving through the rear exit. Whether the process of growing or the process of perishing predominates often depends on what is happening between the doors. If the atmosphere on the inside radiates love, faith, and hope, fewer people lapse into inactivity. Likewise, a spirit of high morale attracts more people through the front door. As a fire ignites anything flammable within reach, so genuine faith sparks a heartfelt response to God among many who live nearby. Without the oxygen of high morale, however, the spiritual flame smolders and dies.

What if a church lacks the fresh imagination of faith? Then it expects little and receives even less. Morale sags and staleness sets in. Repetition produces a gradual lowering of excitement about Jesus Christ. Vivid appreciation of the presence of God gives way to preserving the status quo. Legalism dominates. A fixed way of doing things suppresses any desire for growth and expansion.

Tedium replaces freshness. Outworn forms of church life continue with little measurable effectiveness. Prolonging the nonproductive pattern produces a slow decadence in which apathy numbs any hint of vigorous growth. The members go through the motions of "church," expecting little change in themselves or among their friends and neighbors. Nevertheless, the congregation may experience high survival power; for decadence, undisturbed by the inevitable changes required by brisk growth, is a slow process. The lasting values of the gospel keep slowly ebbing. What remains is the appearance of "church," without any of the realities of the living Christ.

An alternative is available, however. A church may exhaust its ineffective ways and desire something better. The Holy Spirit plants creative springs of originality and God-given hope in the minds of some church leaders. At such a crucial time, the seeds of growth may germinate. New life may spring up in a quick period of transition. Morale begins to build. Joyous progress becomes evident in the number of new Christians and in the quality of spiritual life.

Such a transition is possible only when faith, hope, and prayer precede realization. The adventure of imagining a growing, effective church anticipates its actual development. Church leaders dream of growth to come and then, in due season, arouse themselves to do something about it. Morale builds as they believe God is going to act and then begin acting on their belief. High morale, resulting from exercised faith, is the fruit of experiencing the Holy Spirit's present ministry; but the dreams of faith come first.

Before Martin Luther nailed his ninety-five theses to the Wittenberg Door, he dreamed of church reform. Before George Fox awakened England with his Spirit-filled preaching, he dreamed of transformed lives. Before David Livingstone set sail for Africa, he dreamed of spreading the gospel across the Dark Continent. Before the frontier preachers of the United States planted churches all across the West, they dreamed of making converts in every town and village. Before the growing churches of today started expanding, someone dreamed about the possibility of touching many lives with the redeeming power of Christ. Dreams of faith create the seeds of church growth, for faith by its nature turns God-given dreams into effective action.

A church preserves its vigor as long as it anticipates a real contrast between what has been and what may be. This anticipation leads the congregation to obey the commands of the living Lord. Think of a man confined to a wheelchair who must learn to walk again. His two legs are like faith and obedience. The first step of faith —trust—must give way to the second—obedience. The church taking the initial step of trust expects the living God to cause the growth. The following step of obedience takes the initiative to share God's life-changing gospel. Some people respond, and the church grows.

As the man in the wheelchair begins to walk, he gains confidence that he can take more steps, and yet more. A church that begins to move forward takes courage for more advance. It discovers fresh nerve to venture beyond the safety of the past. The excitement of growth encourages it to make necessary changes. It develops a spirit of high morale. Without the advance of healthy growth, however, only decadence remains. When decline has run its deadening course, a church is in full decay.

Growth is not optional for a church concerned with high morale; it is a necessity. When an airplane is in flight, the instant that the forward thrust ceases, inevitable decline begins. Unless a restoration of power propels the plane to recover the lost altitude, disaster looms ahead. The pilot and crew must keep a sharp eye on the plane's instruments. The danger calls for immediate action. Whatever it takes, they must find an energy source to rebuild the momentum.

High morale supplies fuel for the Holy Spirit to thrust the church forward. As long as the power is on, it moves at a steady pace; but when the energy thrust decreases, the church's growth rate slows. Any decrease in growth momentum signals danger, and the leaders must call for corrective actions at once. Whatever the cost, the church must find a reinstatement of power to rebuild the momentum. The only alternative is decadence and decline. Left unchecked, they lead to disaster and death.

Whenever a growth momentum begins to build, wise leaders will keep it going. People are making an unspoken value judgment; they are voting with their feet. Discerning leaders will sense whether the growth represents heart commitments to Christ or merely more spectators in a building. Once convinced that the growth is not counterfeit, however, wise leaders will pour their efforts into more expansion. As outreach continues, the education and edification efforts of the church will expand to meet the increased need. Rather than trying to consolidate their gains, the pastor and influential lay leaders will work to increase the growth rate. As more and more people receive Christ and his power in their lives, a mounting sense of excitement flows through the congregation.

The message of Christianity becomes a vivid reality for persons who are genuinely converted. Before experiencing Jesus Christ, their search for meaning in life often ended in frustration. What they expected to produce purpose and happiness usually did not. Something vital was missing from their experience. Then they received Christ as Lord and personal Savior in a meaningful conversion. Their inner values changed. They found a personal love that began to grip their lives, unexplainable apart from God. Living faith gave them a new perspective on everyday living.

With all the struggles and temptations, converts yet

conclude that this new life is far better than anything they knew before. They begin to discover spiritual food in the Word of God that nourishes Christian devotion. Their new values find reinforcement in the high commitment of living for someone greater than themselves. If they join a growing church, they find encouragement and a refreshing attitude of love and acceptance. They cannot help but tell their friends and relatives about the recent challenges and changes. As the number of converts like them increase in a church, the sense of fervency and exhilaration spreads. No flame spreads like the fire of new converts.

High morale may well provide a clue to why some churches grow and others do not. Churches that sustain high morale almost always grow. Congregations with low morale usually become stagnant and nongrowing. What builds morale in your church? How do leaders restore lost power? What will establish a climate of excitement and expectancy? What ingredients go into an effective mix of esprit de corps? Definite patterns emerge in high morale, growing churches. This chapter explores three of the key elements: *contagious expectancy, good experiences,* and *God-given achievement.*

CONTAGIOUS EXPECTANCY

Morale builds through a contagious sense of expectancy. In growing churches high expectations flow between people and pastor. The people hold a remarkable sense of confidence in their minister. They like him as a person and as a pastor. They look to their minister for a valuable example of personal warmth

and a Christian life-style. They follow his or her philosophy of ministry with enthusiasm. They expect much
from him and they are seldom disappointed.

Over a period of time they give their minister authority to correspond to his responsibility. As he proves his
God-given leadership, they give him the power to
make crucial decisions in concert with the opinion-
makers of the congregation. They expect their minister
to lead the church. A successful pastor seldom gains
such confidence in fewer than five years. Satisfying relationships result from weeks, months, and years of
faithfulness. What happens in the first five years of a
pastor's tenure makes an interesting study. From a seed
idea in management research, Ronald Allen, a Friends
pastor in Friendswood, Texas, launched his own investigation in the church. Although research is somewhat
tentative at this point, his thesis seems to fit the experience of many.

Allen compares the relationship between people and
pastor to passing a basketball back and forth. If either
side holds the ball, conflict will develop. The conflict, in
turn, can either speed up the process of communicating
expectations or lead to serious trouble. In the first two
years, people and pastor exchange the ball labeled "expectations." They must come to agreement on what
they expect for the church and from each other. The
people pass the ball first, communicating what they
anticipate from their pastor. Far more than a job description, their unspoken desires include what kind of
person they hope he is, what role he will fill in their
personal lives, and what kind of church they expect him
to develop.

Before satisfying relationships can form, the pastor must also communicate his expectations to the people. In a growing church, the minister expects the members to be highly committed. He counts on a hearty response of time, money, and energy to every project and goal designed for the church's good. It takes some time to communicate fully his style of competent Christian living and his system of theology. It takes even more time to inspire people with his dreams for the future. Without a healthy measure of confidence in his hopes coming true, sharing his goals only sets the pastor up for failure. When people and pastor come to a heartfelt agreement on expectations, however, they are ready for the next stage of relationship building.

In the third and fourth years of the pastor's tenure the "status" ball comes into play. In this context the word *status* means respect and esteem and in no way implies self-seeking. As the minister pays the price of faithfulness, the people respond in deep loyalty. In the crises of counseling, marriages, funerals, conversions, and dozens of other pastor-people involvements, the pastor's status builds. In subtle, often nonverbal ways, the people begin to communicate an all-important message: "You are *my* pastor." The minister reciprocates: "You are *my* people." They confer upon each other status, respect, and esteem.

During this time period the wise pastor lets the word out that he is not looking for greener pastures. In his innermost thoughts, he plans to minister to this congregation for the foreseeable future. Within the limits of the denomination's type of church government, he turns down offers to serve in other churches. The peo-

ple in turn express their desire for the pastor to remain
with them indefinitely. An emotional and spiritual marriage binds people and pastor. In the depths of their
souls both sense that they belong to each other. Divorce
is unthinkable.

In the fifth year and thereafter, the ball of "love and
appreciation" enters the game. In this final stage gratitude and affection flow back and forth between people
and pastor in dozens of ways. In print, in sermons, and
in personal conversations, the pastor expresses love for
the people. The members reciprocate with high esteem and tangible tokens of appreciation. If this warm
relationship does not find expression, trouble will follow.

The punch line of Allen's thesis is that the pastor can
lead the church in drastic change only after five years
of a growing relationship. Few churches want major
innovations when a new pastor first arrives. If the congregation is hurting from a recent bad experience, it
may welcome immediate change; but in most churches
conflicts develop because the pastor tries to initiate
change too soon. Major changes in church life usually
require clear expectations, accepted status, and exceptional love. When satisfying relationships are intact, in-
novation becomes far more acceptable. Then people
and pastor move together in a workable unity.

In high-morale churches the interaction between
people and pastor sets the tone as positive, helpful,
supportive. The pastor affirms the people, their gifts,
the church, and its great possibilities and opportunities.
The people support their pastor and are willing to give
generously of their time and energy. They rally behind

his leadership. A beautiful spirit of trust, giving, and love flows between pastor and people in a high-morale church.

The story is told of a little village in an isolated land where the people shared a boundless sense of happiness. Only one feature about their life together was unusual: they engaged in the delightful custom of giving fuzzies to one another. Something about fuzzies felt good and made people happy.

Then one day someone became upset over a petty matter and started a nasty rumor of retaliation. "Have you heard about the coming shortage of fuzzies?" the disgruntled member of the community began asking. Before long, people began hiding their fuzzies. They buried them in fields, hid them in out of the way places, locked them in vaults. Only on birthdays or anniversaries did they wrap up fuzzies as special presents. In time they quit giving them altogether. Suspicion and selfishness triumphed.

The little village became a miserable place to live. People grew sad, gloomy, depressed. Discord and strife broke out. Tension and suspicion replaced the former trust and confidence. Then, one day while some of the children were playing in a field, they stumbled onto a hidden cache of fuzzies. The tingle to their touch felt wonderful. With delighted laughter they gave some to their friends. The more they gave them away, the happier they felt.

The adults soon noticed and remembered the old days. Soon they too joined the fun and brought out their fuzzies from hiding, and the village became an uplifting place to live again. What are fuzzies? Nothing more than heartfelt compliments and sincere appreciation. Not flattery, true fuzzies build up another person's morale. The legend illustrates what can happen between people and pastor in a local congregation.

Expressions of appreciation keep the love-flow moving, but experienced church leaders know that not all problems disappear through tenderness alone. Sometimes love has to get tough with the problem. Often the greatest hindrances to growth are certain problem-producing personalities within the congregation. Internal troubles hinder a church's growth more than anything else. No wonder the New Testament stresses church unity with such vigor (see Matthew 18:15–17, Ephesians 4:3, 1 Peter 3:8). Church leaders will find it impossible to sustain high morale without dealing with problems and problem-producing people.

The style of problem solving, however, varies dramatically with the individual leader. Five pastors deal with problems in five different ways. Each leader has a style that works well for him. Imagine each of the pastors in charge of a swimming hole. Think of the problem producer as someone making waves, disturbing the other swimmers. How does each pastor respond to the crisis?

One pastor calls a meeting of the Ruffled Waters Committee. "I suppose you are all somewhat aware that we have a problem," he begins. He avoids naming those at fault or becoming too specific about the situation; yet he slips in enough hints so that he makes the committee aware of the problem without embarrassing anyone. Along with the glittering generalities, the warmth in his voice communicates a sense of healing. Since he speaks in broad and positive terms, no one else wants to become too specific or critical. Committee members leave the meeting feeling better, but not quite sure about the exact nature of the problem.

In between sessions the pastor does his homework with diligence. He keeps the focus solution-oriented instead of problem-conscious. He talks with individuals in indirect terms about their ideas for solving the problem. Along with asking for their insights, he works out possible solutions himself. If by the next month the troublemaker is still making waves, he brings it to the committee again. This time the discussion is more frank and open, but several options are available. By the third month the solution is at hand.

Another pastor serves a church with several strong personalities, each aggressively pursuing an area of lay ministry. In spite of their good intentions, occasional conflicts arise. If it were his swimming hole, this pastor would go upstream and pour oil on the water. His conciliatory approach centers on love, warmth, and personal friendships. Over a twenty-year period of service his depth of relationships permits him a unique peacekeeping role. Long ago he earned the right to be heard and heeded on any issue. He works consistently at maintaining the confidence the people place in him.

At another church two pastors take almost opposite approaches. If someone were making waves in his swimming hole, the senior pastor would mention it to some of the other swimmers. "I feel terrible that there are waves in our own pond. It makes me sick on the inside to see what is happening. Doesn't it make you feel bad? I don't know what to do!" Guess what happens next? On their own, some people gang up on the wave maker and put a stop to the nonsense. This pastor alerts others to the problem, but he takes a nondirective approach to its solution.

The associate pastor's style is highly directive. If it were his swimming hole, he would wade in with a twinkle in his eye and dunk the troublemaker. With his strong personality he confronts the issue head-on. Sometimes he loses the bout and finds himself dunked, but not often. With a perceptive mind and a clear grasp of issues, he feels comfortable with eyeball-to-eyeball confrontation. His willingness to take the initiative, regardless of the risk, makes him a colorful and controversial leader. Some people love his style; others dislike his tactics intensely, but no one questions his ability to get a following.

The pastor of another church plays a lifeguard role. His faithfulness over the years has earned him full respect in his function. No one doubts his sincerity or good intentions or the intensity of his personal feelings about the trouble. With genuine concern for most of the swimmers' happiness, he blows the whistle on the problem causer. He asks him to step out of the swimming hole for a moment. Then with genuine warmth he puts his arm around the fellow's shoulder, and the two take a little walk. His approach is one-on-one in private.

He smiles and speaks in a soft voice, "We want you to be happy in our swimming hole. We want everyone here to have fun, but it seems obvious that something serious is bothering you. If you are not happy at our swimming hole, there are some fine ones on downstream. Maybe you would like one of them better." He does not run many people off the premises. When, how-

ever, it comes to theological issues that are not up for
compromise or personalities who insist on having their
own way to the detriment of the church as a whole, he
does not hesitate to take action.

Some wave makers move on to other swimming
holes, but not all. Those who choose to stay quit making
waves and adopt a better attitude. One of the beneficial
side effects is what happens to the other swimmers.
They believe in their leader's philosophy and way of
doing things, so they form a team and become a cohesive crew. Solidarity and harmony characterize their
life together. They intend to make their swimming hole
the happiest and best in the whole county.

The analogy illustrates only five styles of problem
solving. Dozens more exist. The crucial element is to
develop an effective way of handling disgruntled people that fits one's gifts, style, and personality. Over a
period of years, why not polish one approach until it
sparkles with success? Then let the Lord use it for the
good of his church, but do not expect instant miracles.
You may not walk on the water, but you can calm the
waves.

Most of the attention in a growing church focuses on
Christ rather than on problems. Morale builds through
a contagious sense of expectancy toward God. Members really believe in Christ's presence among them in
the concrete reality of a personal encounter. Their attitude in approaching worship radiates an electric expectancy: "God is here right now." The people anticipate the Lord's touch to heal personal hurts and grant
Christ's forgiveness. Inspiring music, helpful sermons,
and convicting biblical insights stimulate adoration,

praise, repentance, and prayer. With a positive response to Christ, high-morale churches are filled with his presence.

A natural overflow is that Christians in growing churches share a deep-seated enthusiasm about Jesus Christ. God's supernatural working slips into casual conversations, especially when the topic turns to a personal crisis or the need for guidance. Answered prayer and helpful applications from the Bible cause as much excitement as a recent job promotion or a new baby. Church leaders encourage all who make a new or a renewed profession of faith to declare it in some public way. As the persons go on record before others, they reinforce their recent commitments. Furthermore, by telling of their experiences in receiving Christ, the members give one another permission to speak of spiritual things. The more Christians talk about Christ, the more they reinforce their own faith and the positive feelings of the group.

Behind the conversation lies an intense belief about the gospel's life-changing power. The conviction about the validity of the message to transform morals, heal marriages, and restore values permeates growing churches. The congregation reads about the gospel in Scripture and then experiences it in everyday life. Honest doubts lead to an intense search for satisfying answers. Because of an obedient response to the biblical message, the people feel convinced that life is better now and for all eternity. As a result, they want their friends to find the same kind of help. As the old saying goes, "Nothing beats a satisfied customer."

GOOD EXPERIENCES AND CHURCH QUALITY

A contagious sense of expectancy helps a church grow. It is the first of three key ingredients in building a church's morale, but expectancy cannot be maintained without a repeated pattern of satisfying experiences. Blind faith may start someone down a promising path, but if he stumbles again and again, hopes of reaching his destination will soon disappear. His dreams then evaporate like the morning mist, and he concludes that his path is a confused maze going nowhere. If, however, he makes steady progress step after step, he expects more.

Morale builds through a series of good experiences. Some churches have a track record of good feelings among members. Others specialize in splitting hairs and lifting scalps. It takes little discernment to sense which kind improves morale. What will help a church forge a better set of experiences for its people? I believe good experiences are founded on unselfishness, erected on excellence, and finished with trust.

A deep level of unselfishness sets the foundation. "The church God blesses gets outside of itself," says pastor C. W. Perry of Rose Drive Friends Church in Yorba Linda, California. The concept pervades the church's thinking. His principle applies to every area of Christian service—witnessing, caring, giving. My own investigation adds credibility to Perry's principle. Finances, perhaps more than any other objective indicator, reveal a church's level of unselfishness.

I measured external giving in four churches to see the relationship between growing churches and unselfishness.[1] External giving includes all the money a church gives outside itself for such expenditures as missions, community outreach, benevolences, and denominational assessments. Internal giving, in contrast, reflects what the local church spends to maintain itself on items such as salaries, buildings, and supplies. External giving for these four growing churches averaged 25 percent of their total income. Another study of five growing churches ranging in size from 200 to 2,000 also investigated external and internal giving.[2] The five averaged 19 percent in external giving, far more than most churches. Per capita giving too, in all the congregations of both studies, far exceeded denominational averages.

Growing churches care about God's work in the world and express their concern in tangible ways. Their sacrifice calls for more volunteer labor and scrutinized budgets; yet God honors their faith through the by-product of high morale. Monetary generosity spills over into everything the church does. Evangelism, social service, and a genuine caring about nonmembers flourish when self-giving is the norm. What's more, the unselfish church pleases God. When it comes to providing good experiences, church growth is related to unselfishness.

On the foundation of unselfishness, high-morale churches erect church programs marked by excellence. Although methods vary, pastors and lay leaders in high-morale churches always generate excitement for the church program. The leadership keeps communicating that something good is happening and is going to continue to happen. Then they give themselves to the task

of making it excellent. Why should church leaders set-
tle for anything less than quality in church life? One of
the characteristics of Jesus was the measure of excellence in his ministry. "He has done everything well"
(Mark 7:37, NIV), the people commented. As the church
follows his example, good experiences multiply. Then
intangible feelings like joy and anticipation soon prevail.

To reject excellence as a standard is to invite the
living death of mediocrity. The friend of an old farmer
was telling him about the new county agent. He was
introducing principles and practices that yielded excellent results. "It's amazing," the friend bubbled with
enthusiasm, "what the new methods of farming will
produce." The old farmer seemed unimpressed. "A little new-fangled fertilizer and the crops double," the
friend continued. The farmer showed no response. The
friend refused to give up hope of persuading the recal-
citrant farmer; so with mounting ardor he made a final
plea, "Will you go with me to the next meeting spon-
sored by the county agent?"

"Nah, I ain't goin'," the old farmer replied.

"Why not?"

"Wal, I already know better farmin' than I'm doin'."

Forgetting about the importance of excellence, some
church leaders identify with the old farmer. "Why
exert ourselves further," they wrongly reason, "when
we already know better than we are doing?" The tragedy is that the old farmer went broke after a few years.
Not a few churches are heading for similar disaster. A
deadly danger is for the focus to turn contentedly inward on the present constituents instead of outward to

nonmembers. A church's administrative machinery, for example, may run smoothly, and yet the congregation experiences no growth. Efficiency turned inward on the church's present maintenance is not the same as real excellence.

A series of good experiences is based on unselfishness and built with excellence; yet it will collapse without the finishing touch of genuine trust. As a moral value, trust is on the wane today, and suspicion moves in wherever integrity is lost. Distrust runs rampant in politics, education, and business. The apprehension follows the many sad experiences following moral decay. The present moral decline eroding Christian values in the Western world presents grave consequences. The stability of the economy, the strength of the family, and the survival of basic freedoms stand in jeopardy. It is time for the church to demonstrate a creative alternative.

For morale to increase, the sense of mutual confidence in the church must stand in stark contrast to the outside world. And it can! No other institution on earth holds as great a basis for authentic trust. It emerges from the very nature and mighty acts of the triune God. Christians do trust their Lord and hold absolute values based on his revelation. With a built-in desire to emulate him and follow his teaching, Christians trust one another. When their trust is betrayed, mature Christians put forgiveness into practice. If credibility will not thrive in this setting of dependable fellowship, it is doomed! Unselfishness, excellence, and trust lead to a series of satisfying experiences.

GOD-GIVEN ACHIEVEMENT

The two major principles discussed so far establish the climate for healthy growth. Both contagious expectancy and good experiences contribute to high morale. Expectancy builds positive feelings, and good experiences enhance warm relationships; yet the two will not do by themselves. Something more of God's doing must show in what the church accomplishes. One more principle calls for attention. Without it, even the highest morale will eventually run down.

Morale builds through God-given achievement. Visit any fast-growing church and see for yourself. Watch the smiles light up on the people's faces as you ask the simple question, How are things going at your church? Then step back and listen to an enthusiastic report of God's accomplishments in their midst. In addition to growth, almost any kind of group achievement will increase the morale. A coat of paint, well-cared-for lawns, or any new facility will give the spirits a lift. Excellence in Sunday school, music, or a service project will contribute to the esprit de corps.

Measurable progress toward the church's "owned" goals elevates morale. Church leaders demonstrate that they own a goal by taking action. A growth goal, for example, might require added space and parking, another evangelism staff member, or a second worship service. It might require more Sunday school classes and fellowship groups to incorporate the new people. The church owns the goal only when it expends the time, money, energy, and prayer to add the increments

that make continuous growth possible. Goal achievement serves as such an integral part of high morale that
Ralph R. Bentley and Averno M. Rempel of Purdue
University build it into their definition of the term.
They define morale as "the interest and enthusiasm
that a person displays toward the achievement of individual and group goals in a given situation."[3]

Both individual and group goals need attainment. A
growing church embraces a series of interacting objec-
tives. The members strive together for common goals
that reflect many individual desires. Everyone active in
the church feels one or two of his own dreams is finding
fulfillment. Some will rejoice in the Christian training
of children. Others thrive on the fulfillment of friendship and fellowship needs. Many discover in Christ a
satisfying purpose and meaning in life.

Genuine achievement means a high degree of
spiritual health. The popular theory that growing
churches produce shallow counterfeits of authentic
Christians is seldom if ever true. My research
confirmed what other church-growth investigators had
already learned: that churches with a high evaluation of
spiritual health are sustaining rapid growth rates.[4] Nongrowing churches should view the findings with a sense
of alarm. When a church considers itself quite healthy,
yet shows little interest in growth, the prognosis is only
decline and decay.

On the other hand the congregation with steady
growth senses the vitality of its church. When people
are finding real spiritual help, the word spreads. Perceptive leaders somehow sense the difference between
healthy and counterfeit growth. Their reassuring inner

discernment is no illusion if both the organism and the organization are growing. The relationship between the two is something like the spirit and the body. The organism, like the human spirit, is the real life from God; but it inevitably requires an organizational pattern, analogous to the human body. Of course, if only one develops, the growth pattern is abnormal and unusual.

That growing churches build only a human organization rather than a spiritual organism is a myth. The body of Christ always develops an institutional expression. Without an effective pattern of organized functioning, a church sooner or later strangulates itself. Only when an institution gives way to institutionalism does it betray its true purpose. The problem is one of servant and master. As an institution, the church follows its Lord in the role of servant; but when institutionalism sets in, it assumes the role of master and functions only to serve itself. The sad result of reversing roles is neglect of the gospel and disobeying the mandates of the Lord.

A red flag should fly whenever the growth stops, signaling the danger of institutionalism. Nongrowth most often follows disobedience to the Lord of the church and neglect of the gospel he gave. Whenever a church stops growing, it starts dying. The longer nongrowth persists, the more entrenched institutionalism becomes. Then a most unenviable task faces the church's leaders. To resurrect a dying church is never easy. How much better to keep both the spiritual organism and human organization growing in harmony. Most growing churches do both, and do it well.

Another sign of institutionalism is a continuing decline in the congregation's morale. Self-serving institutions hold little appeal for dynamic Christians; so an occasional morale-check is a good idea. For example, a measurable relationship exists between a church's positive attitudes toward its programs and its growth rate. Donald A. McGavran and Win C. Arn in *How to Grow a Church* suggest a simple survey for that purpose.[5] In my research of four churches, the adapted questionnaire asked worshipers to rate the congregation's programs on a scale. Like a snapshot, the answers pictured the worshiper's morale about church programs at one moment in time. The tabulated results revealed that the morale standings and the growth rate for the last year ranked in the same order.[6]

The church with the highest marks in morale showed the largest percentage gain in membership and attendance for the previous year. The congregation with the next highest morale ranking showed the second highest growth rate. The other two followed in sequence. A similar pattern is evident all across the country. Check your church's morale, and then ask a few growing churches in your community to use the same instrument in measuring their morale. As you compare results, ask the churches with the highest morale some questions. You may discover some insights to increase the morale in your church.

Someone may ask which comes first. Does high morale produce growth, or does a growing church build extraordinary morale? Each affects the other in an upward spiral. It will prove more productive, however, to place the stress on morale first. With careful attention a spirit of joy will become the normal feeling-tone of the congregation. Such a healthy climate stimulates attention to growth. A church with low morale, on the other hand, finds growth efforts difficult and discouraging.

Morale builds through contagious expectancy, good experiences, and God-given achievement. The climate of high morale creates optimum conditions for great growth. But why should a church want more growth? What does "church growth" mean? What commands does Christ expect his people to obey so he will give growth to the church?

NOTES

1. Charles E. Mylander, "Suburban Friends Church Growth: A Study of Four Churches" (Doctor of Ministry thesis, Fuller Theological Seminary, 1975), pp. 115–17.
2. David W. Bennett and James E. Murphy, "Church Growth and Church Health: Diagnosis and Prescription" (Doctor of Ministry thesis, Fuller Theological Seminary, 1974), pp. 78, 84, 89, 99, 105.
3. Interview with Ralph R. Bentley, Measurement and Research Center, Purdue University.
4. Bennet and Murphy, "Church Growth and Church Health," and Mylander, "Suburban Friends Church Growth," pp. 157–74.
5. Donald A. McGavran and Win C. Arn, *How to Grow a Church* (Glendale, Cal.: Regal Books, 1973), pp. 10–11.
6. Mylander, "Suburban Friends Church Growth," pp. 118–19.

2. Follow Christ's Marching Orders

"The indispensable condition for a growing church is
that it wants to grow."
                                        —C. PETER WAGNER

In an unbroken continuity from the New Testament
times until today God's church not only survives but
often grows vigorously. Its expansion becomes evident,
not in a spiritual stratosphere far removed from planet
earth, but in congregations of real people gathered in
the name of Jesus Christ. Human leadership is vital in
any church, but it is never able to add even one person
to the company of the redeemed. Only Jesus Christ can
regenerate a heart and bestow eternal life. Church
leaders must remember that "God . . . causes the
growth" (1 Corinthians 3:7).* In the New Testament the
expectations for church growth are expressed in the
Great Commission, in the Book of Acts, in the principles of Paul, and in the prophecies of the Book of Revelation.

Each worshiping assembly, with the living presence

---

* Biblical quotations in this book are from the New American Standard
  Bible, unless otherwise indicated.

of Jesus Christ in the midst, represents God's church at large. Since your church is part of Christ's church, God is causing your church to grow. Nevertheless, some church leaders do not want their congregations to grow. They fabricate a hundred excuses for maintaining the status quo and resisting the changes that new people will bring. "It is really the quality that counts. Numbers aren't important," some rationalize. "I like our little church just the way it is," others murmur. "It will cost too much money. We can't afford it," a few complain. In reality, however, church leaders who oppose the growth of the church find themselves in the embarrassing position of hindering the grace of God.

If God's people remain faithful, they will take seriously the undeniable imperatives of Scripture. In receptive circumstances such as our own day affords, growth will normally follow from the obedience of faith. What mandates does God expect his people to obey so he can give growth to the church? A mandate is an authoritative command, a directive from a higher authority to a lower one—in other words, marching orders. Four mandates are vital for healthy church growth.

THE GREAT COMMISSION

The first mandate is the Great Commission, the set of marching orders that came from the lips of Jesus just before his ascension. The cross and the resurrection, with all their redemptive significance, lie in the immediate background. The Great Commission forms the climax of the Gospels and the starting point for the Acts of the Apostles. Its position in Jesus' ministry suggests that our Lord himself considered it his supreme mandate. As such, it is the most important directive of all time. The church today can expect God-caused growth only to the extent that it obeys his words.

> All authority has been given to Me in heaven and on earth. Go therefore and make disciples of all the nations, baptizing them in the name of the Father and the Son and the Holy Spirit, teaching thcm to observe all that I commanded you; and lo, I am with you always, even to the end of the age (Matthew 28:18–20).

> Go into all the world and preach the Gospel to all creation (Mark 16:15).

> Thus it is written, that the Christ should suffer and rise again from the dead the third day; and that repentance for forgiveness of sins should be proclaimed in His name to all the nations—beginning from Jerusalem. You are witnesses of these things (Luke 24:46–48).

> You shall receive power when the Holy Spirit has come upon you; and you shall be My witnesses both in Jerusalem, and in all Judea and Samaria, and even to the remotest part of the earth (Acts 1:8).

That a person must receive Christ as his own Lord and Savior before bearing witness to others makes sense. The transition from receiving God's love to proclaiming it to others lies embedded in the gospel itself. This is clearest in the Gospel of John through its theme of "sending." The Father sent his Son Jesus (see John 3:16–17) so that men and women might believe and receive eternal life. Throughout the fourth Gospel Jesus referred to the Father as "the one who sent me."

The climax came when Jesus charged his disciples: "As the Father has sent me, I also send you" (John 20:21). The growing church must not only help its people experience God's love but must send them to proclaim it.

In Matthew's Gospel an expanded text of the Great Commission provides material for careful analysis. Jesus' final marching orders are built on the powerful premise of his authority (Matthew 28:18). While on earth he displayed authority to forgive sins, demonstrating it in healing the diseased and deformed. He claimed authority over the teachings and interpretations of the best scholars of his day. On the basis of his completed redemptive work at the cross and in the resurrection, he claimed all authority in heaven as well as on earth. In other words, he now holds unlimited power to complete his actions and execute his commands.

Jesus' authority shatters the "any religion is good if its adherents are sincere" idea. The following complaint is common among church people. "Yes, we are Christians, but other cultures profess some other religion. Who are we to disturb them? Why not live and let live?" Beneath such talk lies a disturbing fear: "Maybe we Christians are not right; just maybe we are wrong."

Such thinking belies a bit of shallow reasoning. The nature of truth itself repels it. Two opposites cannot both be true. By definition, one is false. Jesus made unrelenting claims as the only way to the Father. Either his claims are true, or they are false. If his stand is true, all contradictory ones are false. Granted, the world religions contain bits and pieces of wonderful truth, but only one way leads to the Father (see John

14:6). The powerful premise of Jesus' authority shatters personal fears of an inadequate gospel.

Jesus next gave a precise precept: "make disciples of all the nations." The only imperative in the original Greek of Matthew 28:18–20 is "make disciples." Church-growth thinkers therefore reject as false the assumption that preaching and witnessing alone will fulfill the Great Commission. It is not enough to see an initial response to the gospel in the form of a decision. Certainly the decision is essential in the disciple-making process, but it is only a first step, not the end of the road. For continuing spiritual development, the person needs to be incorporated into a recognized body of Christian people. Without registering as a member in a Christian church or fellowship, few who make decisions become responsible disciples.

Leaders of the church-growth movement use *disciple* in the original sense it carries in Matthew 28. It conveys the meaning of winning new converts to an ongoing relationship with Jesus Christ. To become a disciple means that a person enters the same relationship with Jesus Christ that the original apostles experienced. The term is a synonym for genuine conversion followed by responsible church membership. It does not indicate somewhat lax Christians who now want to experience the deeper life; nor does it mean fringe members who join a small group with disciplines designed to build Christian character. Rather than discerning various degrees of spiritual maturity, the term *disciple* simply means a genuine Christian.

In the Great Commission in the Book of Matthew the specialized Greek word *ethne* (the "other" nations, peoples, ethnic groups) is used instead of *laos* (the people of the covenant). The direction in mission is outward. Full obedience to the Great Commission will result in extensive church growth among every nation, language, people, tribe, and kinship group. It will mean planting new churches in every culture. The people of God will make disciples, not only of people in faraway places around the world, but also of their near neighbors. The church has often crossed land and sea to make one convert while ignoring receptive groups of people in its own community. More than one denomination needs to apply cross-cultural church-planting approaches developed on the mission fields to the ethnic enclaves within their home countries.

Three productive processes supplement Jesus' command to disciple the peoples. Going, baptizing, and teaching become means to the end of making disciples. Literally, the "go" of Jesus' command is "going." An accurate translation is "when you go," or "as you go." Jesus *assumes* the going as a first and essential step. The center of attention focuses on making disciples wherever in the world the Lord places each of his people. No Christian dare feel content to send others as foreign missionaries while refusing to "make disciples" at home.

The Lord himself knows how to arrange what Elton Trueblood calls "a redemptive connection." He makes the geographic location, crucial timing, and receptive circumstances intersect for a divine encounter between his messenger and a winnable group of people. The "going" part of the disciple-making process then leads to becoming a recognized member of the body of

Christ, "baptizing them in the name of the Father and the Son and the Holy Spirit" (Matthew 28:19). Regardless of theological differences, all denominations see baptism as part of entering the fellowship of Christ's church. The Friends, my own denomination, emphasize the Spirit's baptism. Other denominations use various forms and modes for baptizing. All agree, however, that Christian baptism has to do with the initial incorporation in the body of Christ.

The third process, "teaching them to observe all that I have commanded you" (Matthew 28:20), relates closely to the central imperative to make disciples of the unconverted. The first disciples joined teaching to their preaching of repentance (see Mark 6:12, 30). Likewise, the proclamation of Jesus included teaching that *preceded* repentance. In the context of the Great Commission, teaching means helping people understand the commitment they are making. Those who hear the gospel have the right to know what following Jesus involves. Becoming a disciple calls for a full commitment to obey his commands. Leading a person to a Christian decision without a heartfelt pledge to live under Jesus' Lordship is sharing only half a gospel.

The Christian teacher dare not miss the primary task, teaching people to obey Jesus. Accumulating knowledge for the sake of learning is a Greek ideal, not a Christian one. The Christian idea calls for knowledge of God with *obedience*. Of course, obedience cannot become a way of life unless one learns what Jesus said and meant. The key in making disciples is unmistakable teaching about an obedient will. Before conversion, a potential convert need not understand or even know everything Jesus taught, but he must accept a personal obligation to obey the Lord without reservation.

Jesus concluded the Great Commission with a precious promise: "I am with you always, even to the end of the age" (Matthew 28:20). In my mind I hear him say, "I am with you at all times, under every possible condition. When everything is going well and when everything is going wrong, I am with you. When people respond in great numbers, and when they simply ignore you, I am with you. When you succeed in carrying out my mandate, and when you die trying, I am with you. When people praise you for your service, and when they slander you behind your back, I am with you. When those to whom you witness accept you, and when they reject you, I am with you."

When confronted with the Great Commission, church leaders often respond, "Yes, but we must become more prepared first. Yes, but we must change the mood first. We must work for social justice first. We must renew the church and revive the present Christians first." "Yes, buts" will never do. Jesus said, "Disciple all the peoples. All authority is mine, and I am with you." Hear the tone of victory and climax in his voice. The spiritual war yet rages, but Christ and his people will overcome. They will fulfill the Great Commission together. Victory is assured!

THE GREAT COMMANDMENT

To love God without reservation, is the second mandate. "You shall love the Lord your God with all your heart, and with all your soul, and with all your mind"

(Matthew 22:37, quoting Deuteronomy 6:5). An un-
qualified love for God is the reasonable response for all
who have experienced his mercy and grace. Fulfilling
the Great Commandment requires more than senti-
mentalism, even more than sincerity. It calls for a heart
set upon doing the Father's will. The more one loves
God, the more meaningful faith becomes as the moti-
vating desire of one's life. The more a congregation
loves God together, the more it possesses the qualities
that contribute to dynamic growth. Qualities such as
profound meaning, high morale, and spiritual intensity
lead to wide expansion of the church.

Intensity of belief and action often result from loving
God without reservation. Intensity makes a striking
difference between a good church and a great church.
A good church believes in Jesus Christ; a great church
believes with intensity. A good church prays; a great
church prays intensely. A good church gives God
thanks; a great church radiates his praise in happy
smiles and joyous singing. A good church serves God; a
great church delights in pleasing him in their con-
certed actions. A good church worships and studies; a
great church puts such joy and intensity into its devotion that its love for God overflows.

The Great Commandment calls for individuals to respond wholeheartedly in both heart and mind. In a
personal life of devotion they keep their heart tender
to Christ, their conscience sensitive to the Holy Spirit.
Every day they yield themselves afresh to the Creator
and Redeemer with a heart full of adoration and praise.
At the same time they give the Lord their mind as a
vehicle of love. Far from turning off their intelligence,

genuine love compels them to use their best mental efforts. In the discipline of study they will learn more of God's revelation in Scripture. If they are wise, they will also benefit by the writings of the great thinkers in the church. They will let great minds who love Jesus help them deal with intellectual problems with honesty and reverence.

THE GREAT COMMITMENT

Something about loving God spills over into caring for others. Nowhere is God's kind of love more natural than among like-minded believers. One of the repeated themes of Scripture is the love Christians show other members of God's family. Jesus called this mandate a new commandment and put it on a par with the Ten. For the sake of alliteration I call it the Great Commitment. It compels the company of the committed to care for one another even to the point of death. No quality is more missing in contemporary society nor more attractive to the non-Christian.

A new commandment I give to you, that you love one another, even as I have loved you, that you also love one another. By this all men will know that you are My disciples, if you have love for one another (John 13: 34-35).

This is My commandment, that you love one another, just as I have loved you (John 15:12).

This I command you, that you love one another (John 15: 17).

Now as to the love of the brethren, you have no need for any one to write to you, for you yourselves are taught by God to love one another (1 Thessalonians 4:9).

Let love of the brethren continues (Hebrews 13:1).

Since you have in obedience to the truth purified your souls for a sincere love of the brethren, fervently love one another from the heart (1 Peter 1:22).

We know love by this, that He laid down His life for us; and we ought to lay down our lives for the brethren (1 John 3:16).

Showing love to other Christians takes on countless forms. In growing churches it often finds expression in cells of Christians. A cell is a fellowship group that is small enough so that the members can hold one another accountable for the disciplines of ongoing discipleship. Multiplying cell life, both spontaneous and organized, is characteristic of growing churches. (In chapter 4 this important secret of church growth will be examined in some detail.) The love-flow between committed Christians in a church makes an indelible impression on the unchurched. Visitors to growing churches put it in their own terms.

"There's a real warmth among your people. I feel it."
"You have such a sense of joy in this church."
"Your people are so friendly."
"The enthusiasm is contagious."

People sense a loving attitude of warmth and acceptance as if it were a fragrant perfume in the air. Someone might object that what is happening amounts to mere sociability. Couldn't a person experience the same feeling with a service club or at a public school

function? The Christian answer is no, not if the supernatural dynamics of the Great Commitment are operat-
ing in full force. The love-flow among Christ's disciples
produces a kind of spiritual help and healing more eas-
ily experienced than described. The result becomes evident in the long-range effect more than in the immediate feeling; yet people intuitively sense genuine
Christian love when they encounter it.

Dietrich Bonhoeffer distinguished between the love
of Christian community and mere human relationships
in his devotional book *Life Together.* "A marriage, a
family, a friendship, is quite conscious of the limitations
of its community-building power; such relationships
know very well, if they are sound, where the human
element stops and the spiritual begins."[1] At the most
profound level neither good feelings nor uplifting experiences bind the church together. Instead, it is
". . . faith working through love" (Galatians 5:6). The
good experiences enriching the fellowship are not the
cause but the effect of sacrificial love flowing among
fellow disciples. As Christ's love flows, his power to
change lives is released. Then Christians who find help
readily tell their unchurched friends about its source.

THE GREAT CONCERN

Heartfelt response to God's love proclaimed in the
Great Commission does not limit itself to other Christians. It begins with the devotional and intellectual disciplines of the Great Commandment, then moves to
the relational dimensions of the Great Commitment,
but does not stop there. Two precise commands from

Jesus summarize the final mandate: "Love your neighbor . . . and your enemy." The Great Concern pertains to how Christians live in the midst of the world system of this evil age. The outward life of service is developed in the midst of a hostile world. Its concern reaches to all the relationships outside the Christian community. The Great Concern differs from the Great Commitment in that it calls for love and holy living in the unbelieving world.

> You shall love your neighbor as yourself (Matthew 22:39, quoting Leviticus 19:18).

> Fill the earth, and subdue it; and rule over [all creation] (Genesis 1:28).

> But let justice roll down like waters and righteousness like an ever-flowing stream (Amos 5:24).

> Love your enemies, and pray for those who persecute you (Matthew 5:44).

The Great Concern captures both the ethical imperative in Scripture and the call for justice and righteousness. It applies also to everything the Bible says about humankind's relationship to the created order, from ecology to social institutions. Committed Christians appear as lights ". . . *in the midst of* a crooked and perverse generation" (Philippians 2:15). On the one hand, Christ's people are delivered out of this present, evil age (see Galatians 1:4). They no longer share its condemnation (see 1 Corinthians 2:6). They hold different moral and spiritual values (see 1 John 2:15–17, John 17:16). On the other hand, they yet live "in the world" with no command to withdraw or isolate themselves (see John

17:13–15). *In the midst of* the world the Lord's people
bear their witness and exert an effective influence for
Christ.

On an individual or family basis, loving one's neighbors and enemies is essential for a church's growth. In
the face of persistent, self-giving love, even enemies
sometimes drop their antagonism. Friendship and love
make it possible for non-Christians to hear the gospel
with the inner ear of the soul. Some respond positively.
Their personal relationship with a Christian friend then
enables the new believer to bridge the gap from secular
life to the church. Unfortunately, the lack of a personal
relationship of genuine friendship is often the missing
bridge of effective evangelism. Friendship bridges can
span the "follow-up gap" between an initial decision
and responsible discipleship.

The rub comes in loving the enemies of one's nation,
or the other side of a labor-management dispute, or the
unjust provocateurs in racial tensions. Then the church
or any individual Christian who takes the Great Concern seriously encounters overwhelming resistance;
yet only a fool would take scissors and cut "love your
enemy" out of Jesus' teachings. Even the thought is
abhorrent! As a Christian ideal, the teaching receives
great admiration and lip service, but the temptation
silently to ignore it remains strong. All such attempts to
edit it out of Christian practice must meet with stead-
fast rejection.

Even when following all four mandates, a congregation must check its message for possible distortion. Is it
showing God's love or only a human facsimile? If all the
emphasis falls on any one set of marching orders, the

church will surely stop growing; yet if a church skips any mandate, it betrays the gospel. Continued stress of God's love brings both focus and balance to the other emphases. On the one hand, God's love leads his people to show by their deeds a genuine alternative to the values of a secular culture. On the other, a high priority given to proclaiming God's love by word gives a healthy balance to other legitimate concerns.

In our complex times committed Christians must beware of canceling out one another's concerns. Some Christians will feel one of the mandates is the most important; others will stress another. Each group must recognize the Lord's commands for the other's activities. Then the various members of the body of Christ can move ahead with mutual support rather than suppressed distrust. A balanced church will stress all four mandates. Since all come from Jesus, all are vital. In him comes the unity for all the marching orders to work in harmony instead of discord.

Church-growth thinkers, focusing on the expansion of the congregation, emphasize effective evangelism. What marks off church-growth strategy from almost all other evangelistic plans is the attention to ends instead of means. House-to-house visitation, city-wide crusades, personal witnessing, and revival meetings are all *methods.* Church-growth thinkers view the variety of methods as only means to an end, not the end itself. They strive to remove every hindrance from the *goal* of evangelism—the growth of the body of Christ (see Colossians 2:19, Matthew 16:18); yet they desire a healthy body, responsive to the head, and not a multiplication of cells without design or direction. The goal of effective evangelism requires obedience to the head of the church who gave the four mandates.

A DESCRIPTION OF CHURCH GROWTH

What is church growth in its fullest and healthiest sense? Four types of development are experienced by a balanced church, and all four are ongoing functions in a healthy congregation. Type one is *internal growth*—everything of spiritual value happening to the members of a church. The broadest of the four categories, it includes spiritual nurture and the conversion of unregenerated church members.

Spiritual nurture includes prayer, church renewal, Bible study, *koinonia,* social service, and a host of other activities. Growth in this sense means progress toward Christian maturity. Internal growth also means leading people within the present membership to a personal encounter with Jesus Christ. Some members attend worship, feel comfortable in ecclesiastical settings, and speak church jargon; yet in the depths of their hearts, they still belong to the kingdom of darkness. They need a new birth, although their names appear on the membership rolls. This kind of internal growth counts for eternity, although human statistics may never reveal it.

Type two is *expansion growth*—adding members to the local church. Most church-growth researchers count only full members in good standing. Within the same denomination similar qualifications and procedures for joining the church often prevail; yet church membership standards sometimes vary too much for meaningful comparison. In my research, for example, I

encountered a major problem with using only membership for comparison. Two of the churches I studied held
a vastly different philosophy of membership. Member-
ship-growth graphs of the two churches did not reflect
their comparative size and strength accurately.

Anyone who knew the churches firsthand would recognize that the largest and strongest had a rather small
membership roll; yet the smallest of the four churches
under study, in terms of actual attendance, kept the
most members on its books. After experimenting with
several formulas, I discovered that the simple average
of membership, worship attendance, and Sunday
school attendance gives a more nearly accurate por-
trayal of a church's actual growth. C. Peter Wagner, an
acknowledged church-growth expert, helped me name
it "composite membership." To calculate composite
membership, for a given year add together the components of adult membership, the twelve-month morning
worship average attendance, and the twelve-month
Sunday school average attendance. Then divide by
three for the composite membership for the year.
When you arrive at the result, you may have to deny
your emotions and let your tough-mindedness rule.

The composite-membership method of calculating
growth appears less flattering for most churches; yet it
assesses their actual growth and strength much better
than ordinary membership alone. To visualize the
growth trends, chart the components of composite
growth for the past ten years on ordinary graph paper
(see appendix, p. 140, for an example). The result will
help the growth analyst as much as the electrocardio-
gram assists a medical doctor. The first line represents
full members. The second and third represent year-

round averages of morning worship and Sunday school. A fourth line, broken or a different color, shows the simple average of the three, or composite membership. At a glance the chart shows a church's growth patterns.

After thinking about the expansion of a local congregation, contrast it with the kind of growth that develops from church planting. *Extension growth* is the third type of church growth—starting new churches that become self-supporting congregations. Unfortunately, church leaders neglect it more than any other type of church growth on the contemporary scene. Research around the world, however, indicates that without church planting a denomination will stop expanding and thus curtail its influence for Christ. Numerous church leaders point to the approximately 333,000 congregations in the United States alone and asked, "Do we really need more churches?" An honest question deserves a careful answer, and the answer is yes!

The present number is only half enough, for several reasons. First, present churches are not reaching all the winnable people. In the United States 95 percent of the churches average less than 350 worshipers on Sunday morning, and 50 percent average 75 or less! According to the number of adherents reported by the present congregations, more than 80 million people remain unchurched. Some are resistant, but many are winnable. The growth of new churches planted throughout the country shows that more congregations will indeed lead many unreached people to Christ. If, however, each new church follows the attendance pattern of the present ones, it will take twice as many congregations to "make disciples" of the present population.

Second, some states and counties in the United States

have far fewer churches than others. The percentage of
unchurched people in the various states reflects the
uneven scattering of churches. According to a 1971
study by the Glenmary Research Center, eight states
show 50 percent or more of their population with no
church affiliation.[2] (They are, from least church affiliation to greatest, Washington, Oregon, California, Ha-
waii, Alaska, Nevada, West Virginia, and Colorado.)
Thirty more states reveal a 35 percent or more unchurched population. These states, along with new
communities and growing population centers throughout the country, desperately need new churches
planted. Static population areas can also benefit by new
churches, especially if they offer unique services and a
style of worship not provided by the present congregations.

Stress on new church evangelism flies in the face of
the current trend of merging separate congregations
into a single church. Careful observers notice that the
merger of two local churches most often produces a
decline in the total membership. In many cases, after
a year or two the combined congregation numbers few
more than the larger of the two churches before the
merger. By way of contrast, a mother church that spins
off a daughter congregation nearly always produces
more total members. The fear that competition from a
new church will destroy the growth of an established
congregation has little basis in fact. More often, the
excitement of several growing churches in a community tends to increase the responsiveness of the unreached. In many instances daughter congregations
help the mother church grow all the more.

The fourth type of church growth is *bridging growth* —crossing cultural barriers in order to plant churches. Most Christians think at once of foreign missions in a distant country, but bridging growth stresses ethnic and linguistic distinctives rather than geographical distance or national boundaries. The traditional label of "foreign missions" does not always fit. Launching a Filipino-speaking congregation in the heart of Los Angeles, for example, requires much the same understanding of language and culture as planting one in the heart of the Phillipines; yet a far greater number of non-Christians remain "across the seas."

The world missions scholar Ralph D. Winter revealed some shocking facts at the 1974 International Congress on World Evangelism in Lausanne, Switzerland.[3] Three massive blocks of humanity remain largely unchurched: the mainland Chinese, the Hindus, who live primarily in South Asia, and the Muslims, who are concentrated in the Middle East, South and Southeast Asia, and Africa. Add the many tribal peoples surrounded by complex cultural barriers, and the enormous size of the unfinished missionary task comes into view. Winter disclosed the startling information that ordinary evangelistic methods, not bridging growth, will result in numerous churches for only 16 percent of the world population. Only crosscultural church planting will effectively evangelize the remaining 84 percent. If every Christian in the world led his friends and neighbors to Christ, more than 2 billion non-Christians would still be left. The need for bridging growth to "make disciples of *all the peoples*" remains staggering.

A DEFINITION OF CHURCH GROWTH

The four types of growth together constitute a broad description of what "church growth" means. But a communication gap still exists. On the one hand, some associate it with scalp-hunting, the numbers game, or the success syndrome, and they pronounce it idolatrous. On the other, some use the term interchangeably with effective Christian education, good church management, or anything beneficial a congregation is doing, and thus they water it down to meaninglessness. Therefore, a precise definition is essential. Here is my attempt.

> Church growth is effective evangelism
> resulting in a numerical increase
> of regenerated Christians
> in local congregations.

Effective evangelism is a workable synonym for church growth. It means presenting the gospel of Christ in such a way that some people respond in the obedience of faith. It suggests the exciting results of transformed lives. To church-growth thinkers, effective evangelism means making disciples, not merely recording decisions. It puts emphasis on incorporation in the church as the normal life-style of Christian discipleship. If incorporation continues at a healthy pace, the number of responsible church members will increase.

Resulting in a numerical increase reflects the unabashed pragmatism of church-growth leaders. They call attention to reaping, rather than sowing. No farmer counts the number of seeds planted in hopes of a crop, but everyone measures the size of the harvest. Likewise, discerning church leaders will measure growth in terms of numerical increase. An accurate accounting serves to stimulate responsible leaders to better stewardship of their outreach efforts. Almost every church keeps accurate records of its income and expenditures. Are church leaders any less responsible for measuring progress or decline in membership and attendance?

Lest church-growth advocates sound too mechanical in applying growth principles, they also emphasize *regeneration.* Only God regenerates a person. The Holy Spirit in a decisive act applies the atoning work of Jesus Christ in his death and resurrection to a person's fallen human nature. The new beneficiary of the forgiveness of sins and the promise of eternal life finds his relationship with God transformed. The convert now follows Jesus Christ in a life of discipleship. Church-growth researchers understand that not every church member is a regenerated Christian, but the phrase accents the goal of effective evangelism, namely, genuine Christians.

In local congregations reflects a high view of the church. It is an essential part of God's plan for making disciples and developing maturity in believers. Each congregation is in local expression "the church of God which He purchased with His own blood" (Acts 20:28). Regenerated Christians, then, do not function in isolation but belong to Christ and to one another. They form one body in Christ with mutual gifts and responsibilities (see 1 Corinthians 12, Romans 12, Ephesians 4). They love and serve as responsible members in local congregations. What Christ is doing in his church as a whole is best seen in local congregations—visible, tangible, measurable.

CHURCH GROWTH AND SPIRITUAL AWAKENING

Most people today view the church as a static institution. In Europe and the United States the influence of the church on everyday life appears less and less effective. Most noticeable is the crumbling of moral values. The present phenomenon is fundamentally different from breaking accepted codes of conduct. Underlying the outward decline is a rejection of Christian values and the very idea of a moral law. When everything becomes relevant, including truth itself, society has no moorings, no roots, no footings.

The moral breakdown touches every facet of human life. Broken homes shatter young lives with emotional trauma. Crime ravages not only inner cities but suburbs and small towns. Dishonesty and greed undermine the economic system. Sexual immorality inflicts terrible psychological damage. Racism raises its ugly head of injustice. Respect for human life dwindles as the blood of aborted babies cries out from the ground. Most frightening of all is the attitude of the rank and file: "I don't care. Just leave me alone." Jesus predicted such a backlash of apathy when he said, "Because of the increase of wickedness, the love of most will grow cold" (Matthew 24:12, NIV).

Moral decline, however, is accompanied by a renewed interest in the supernatural. In any secular bookstore, extensive sections are devoted to works on astrology and the occult. Books on meditation and non-

Christian religions fill up more racks. At the same time an extraordinary interest in the Bible and excellent Christian literature is gaining momentum. Bookshop owners keep a large stock of material on the supernatural for only one reason—customer demand. The desire for supernatural help with life's struggles reflects the common despair with human solutions. Optimistic promises of spiritual progress by human achievement taste sweet but turn bitter in the stomach.

Remarkable breakthroughs in technology and medical science help the outward person immensely. The fruit of applied research adds numerous conveniences to daily life, but the search for inner meaning and freedom from guilt is not satisfied with human answers. In the midst of material prosperity, millions of people remain spiritually famished. Astrology, the occult, and self-imposed meditation fail to quench the thirst caused by sin and separation from God. The churches, in spite of their weaknesses, still offer the only gospel that satisfies the aching hunger of the human heart and mind.

In spite of what most people think, an increasing number of churches are far from static. Thousands of congregations embraced the church renewal movement of the last few decades. For many, its positive repercussions were like a cool breeze on a scorching day. On the theological level, church confessions, preaching, and teaching are more biblical today than they have been for many decades. On the congregational level, lay persons sense the need to serve as players in the game and not sit as spectators in the grandstands. On the personal level, thousands of church members have experienced a fresh commitment to

Jesus Christ. Today most committed Christians view their churches as the only hope for a society in decay.

Fortunately, the church is no longer the whipping boy for poor jokes. Sincere Christians speak about their churches and their values with gripping seriousness. More and more often God's people are forced to take an unmistakable stand for Christian morality and against dishonesty and indecency. The hazy grays of nominal Christianity are disappearing like the morning fog, and light and darkness contrast more starkly all the time. The stage is set for two wonderful developments. Although I claim to be neither a prophet nor the son of a prophet, I believe both will happen before Christ's return to earth.

One breakthrough will be a great moral and spiritual awakening instigated by God's Holy Spirit. Every student of church history knows of the Great Awakening in England and the American colonies during the eighteenth century. The preaching of John Wesley and George Whitefield gave England a new breath of life. In all probability it saved the nation from a bloodbath such as the French Revolution. In the American colonies the powerful preaching of Jonathan Edwards and like-minded men awakened thousands to the things of God. The mighty movement of God's Spirit around 1740 molded the various groups of immigrants into a cohesive people. America as a people was born in the Great Awakening, several decades before the Declaration of Independence.

Some sixty years later, around the turn of the century, a fresh awakening swept the United States. Churches filled with people seeking God's transforming touch upon their lives. Open confession of sin and tangible restitution for past wrongs revealed the extent of the Spirit's moving. Parallel movements occurred in parts of Switzerland, Norway, Scotland, the Netherlands, and France. A similar revival movement awakened churches in the United States in 1831–32. Evangelical awakenings of such a magnitude spawn social and spiritual change of lasting consequence. The awakenings launched movements concerned with slavery, prison abuses, medical care, education, and labor reforms. The modern missionary movement received a mighty forward impetus.

In 1858–59 a powerful awakening turned the developing United States toward God, not just on the frontiers but throughout the land. Dozens of pastors and evangelists, including such famous men as Henry Ward Beecher and Charles G. Finney, preached daily. Churches, auditoriums, and halls across the land opened each noon hour for prayer. Not just on Sundays, but every night people filled churches to capacity to hear the Word of God. In the few short years following 1857 a million converts swept into the churches. The revival accomplished great good, but it did not solve every grievous problem. For example, the powerful preaching against slavery by Finney and others did not result in immediate freedom for blacks. Nevertheless, tremendous progress toward freedom was achieved.

Parallel movements in the United Kingdom reaped a harvest of another million converts. Ireland, Wales, Scotland, England, and numerous European countries felt the impact. Movements in parts of India, Africa, and the West Indies brought thousands to Christ. Most

of those responding became responsible citizens in
many walks of life. Most notable was the worldwide
influence of a fresh wave of missionaries around the
world. Their efforts, along with the pioneers before
them, established crucial beachheads for Christ on
every continent. Less than a century later, Christianity
was gaining more converts every day than any other
religion in the world.

The last great awakening among all the churches in
the United States swept the land in 1905. It followed the
remarkable 1904 revival in Wales under the persuasive
preaching of Evan Roberts. Church history texts often
miss this wave of revival, but more recent historians
know its influence on the American churches. Like
each of the earlier spiritual and moral awakenings, it
sparked an intense desire among non-Christians to hear
the Word of God. With deep conviction of sin and thor-
ough repentance came abounding joy. In 1905 evangelistic efforts were coordinated with unusual ease and
willingness.

In the United States awakenings have often come in
intervals of fifty or sixty years. In most instances they
began during a time of moral decline in the country as
a whole. Grieved with the decay of decency around
them, committed Christians gathered for Bible study
and called out to God in prayer. Some interceded for
revival over a period of months and even years. At the
proper moment their faith and the Holy Spirit's timing
intersected. Then the awakening struck, catching most
other people by surprise. While no one can time the
Spirit's movements, it seems that after seventy-plus
years (1905 to the present) the Western world is over-
due for another evangelical awakening.

To the discerning Christian signs of an impending awakening appear on every side. The moral decline is evident, but so also is the increased concern of the committed. The quality of church life, especially among evangelicals, seems more vigorous than in many decades. While many church members slumber in apathy, the leaders and young people are on the move. The wholehearted commitment of Christian youth provides cause for great rejoicing. With no hint of embarrassment, young people today are taking an open and outspoken stand for Jesus Christ. From an adult perspective they appear fearless in making him known to friends and relatives.

Many discerning church leaders sense the stirrings of God's Spirit on other fronts. In the fields of government, sports, and entertainment a remarkable number of people are turning to Christ and making their Christian testimony public. Some also display public opposition to the current moral decay, even to the point of putting their careers on the line, but the famous and prominent are only the tip of the iceberg. Unseen by most eyes is a grass roots movement reported by the evangelist Billy Graham in his book *How to Be Born Again.* "We now estimate that there are over two million prayer groups and Bible study groups meeting in homes and churches that were not meeting ten years ago."[4] If the estimate is anywhere close to accurate, hope for a genuine awakening abounds.

When Christians really pray with hearts and minds open to God's Word, the Holy Spirit can act in power. I believe a great awakening is coming, but nothing in the teachings of Jesus or any part of Scripture will allow the company of the committed to sit on their hands and wait. Although prayer for a great outpouring of the Holy Spirit is imperative, it will not substitute for hard work. The cry for a great spiritual and moral awakening dare not turn into an excuse to neglect effective evangelism. Indeed, a fresh awakening is most apt to come when God's people obey Christ's commands in wholehearted trust. The call to make disciples who care about justice and righteousness is more urgent than ever. I believe committed Christians are responding and that another development in Christ's church is imminent.

The second breakthrough for churches in the near future may well precede the first. It will come in an unprecedented wave of church growth. While some churches will remain static or decline, most will expand and grow stronger. The demise of the institutional church is nowhere in sight. Already the church growth movement is gaining momentum. At the same time nearly every denomination is giving fresh emphasis to evangelism, with the desire to become effective in making genuine disciples of Jesus Christ. With growth in quality and quantity will come an increased influence to turn the moral tide.

Dozens of churches in every part of the United States right now are bursting with new people and renewed vigor. Almost all are both evangelical and evangelistic, yet they represent most denominations. Most place a major emphasis on Bible teaching and preaching. Without exception they are building relationship bridges to neighbors and friends. Their focus is outward rather then inward. Hundreds of other congregations will catch their secrets in the years to come. God is not capricious in his grace. He is willing to give growth to other churches who will seek it at any cost.

A congregation must pay the price for growth, including the painful process of change. Already many congregations are gearing up for an increased harvest, and more will join their number. Every congregation needs a full system for evangelism and church growth. Churches put dozens of hours into choir rehearsals and sermon preparation for worship. In Christian education, hundreds of volunteer hours go into teaching children, youth, and adults. Youth activities and service projects require extensive time and effort. Most static churches, however, put little time, energy, and money into making disciples from among the unconverted.

The pendulum, however, is swinging. The amount of time and energy devoted to outreach is on the increase. More and more churches are developing systems of training and deploying witnesses on a weekly basis. A few churches are hiring full time staff members for evangelism and discipleship. Growing churches are finding ways of folding God's newfound "lost sheep." More churches are learning how to teach basic Christianity as both belief and life-style. The most successful devote hundred of hours to the task of incorporating new people into an ongoing life of discipleship.

Human leaders working as God's co-laborers are vital if Christ's marching orders are to be fulfilled. What kind of leaders are needed for an effective evangelism/church-growth system? What roles and gifts fit them for their task? What will motivate them to reach others for

Christ and the church? The next chapter will answer
these questions. It will help you mobilize more growth-
producing people in your congregation. What's more,
it may help you discover your own role in church
growth.

NOTES

1. Dietrich Bonhoeffer, *Life Together* (New York: Harper & Row, 1954),
   p. 38.
2. Douglas W. Johnson, Paul R. Picard and Bernard Quinn, "Percent of
   Population Unchurched by Counties in the United States: 1971," a map
   based on data from *Churches and Church Membership in the United
   States: 1971* (Washington, D.C.: Glenmary Research Center). The map
   is available from the Publications Office, United States Catholic Conference, 1312 Massachusetts Ave., NW, Washington, D.C. 20005, and the
   Glenmary Research Center, 4600 East-West Highway, Washington,
   D.C. 20014.
3. Ralph D. Winter, "The Highest Priority: Cross-Cultural Evangelism," in
   Let the Earth Hear His Voice, ed. J. D. Douglas (Minneapolis, Minn.:
   World Wide Publications, 1975), pp. 213–41. Dr. Winter has revised the
   percentages given in the original papers to the percentages cited here.
   The updated statistics are available from The World Mission Center,
   1605 E. Elizabeth Street, Pasadena, Cal. 91104.
4. Billy Graham, *How to Be Born Again* (Waco, Tex.: Word Books, 1977),
   p. 62.

3. Discover Your Role in Church Growth

"The lay ministry is a great idea, but it will not do itself; it will not emerge in power unless it is consciously and deliberately encouraged. . . ."

—D. ELTON TRUEBLOOD

Around the world committed lay persons in countless churches are exercising their God-given ministry. The Holy Spirit will work through these stalwarts in a unique way to help others. The liberating idea of an effective lay ministry is gaining momentum. What's so healthy about these emerging volunteer leaders is their updated understanding of the body of Christ. Each member has a special function and a unique contribution to make. Every Christian needs his fellow believers. All the members in Christ's body depend on one another, or they function inadequately.

In practical experience a parallel truth to the idea of the lay ministry is gaining strength. The secret of a well-mobilized laity lies in the pastors and church leaders who recruit, encourage, and train. These equippers function as the ligaments that coordinate the body (see Ephesians 4:16). Their leadership role is indispensable, and their task of mobilizing unpaid leaders is especially

important. Without such coordinating efforts any
church will flounder. The major thrust of this chapter
concerns unpaid volunteers, but first consider an important insight about paid church-staff members.

A GROWTH-PRODUCING RATIO

The right number of capable equippers supplies an
essential key to church growth. Careful research has
documented a crucial growth ratio between full-time
equippers and actual attendance. The rule of thumb is
(1 + 1): 200, which means one pastor and one secretary
for each 200 people in attendance. When a church
reaches 200 in Sunday school attendance for each pastor supported by a full-time secretary, attendance will
level off. Behind the ratio stands a monumental piece
of research by the religious sociologist Richard A.
Myers. With the help of a computer he analyzed 3,000
churches from twenty denominations in 1958. In 1967
he made a new study with information collected from
6,000 additional churches.

Two of Myers's finding are of particular interest.
First, he showed the need for a full-time secretary or
support person working with each minister. Without
clerical help, a minister becomes too bogged down in
detail to work with maximum effectiveness. A giant
step forward for most smaller churches is to hire a capable secretary who works at least thirty hours a week.
Larger churches may support their pastors with ad-
ministrators, receptionists, or interns. In calculating the
ratio, however, it is unfair to include the pastor's wife
as an additional staff member.

Second, Myers did not count custodians, church musicians, or teachers of day schools on the premises. Only growth-producing staff members backed by able secretaries enter the ratio. The single exception is a director of music who launches several choirs for various age groups. The number of large and small musical groups he initiates may often result in additional growth. The (1 + 1): 200 figure serves as a guide to the maximum expected. When the church nears the ratio, growth will often level off unless the congregation hires another staff member. For outstanding effectiveness, the additional staff person should lead the church's evangelistic thrust!

Myers found a direct relationship among the number of paid staff members, the number of Sunday school classes, and church growth. Each church needs a minimum of ten Sunday school classes, for every full-time minister. The ratio assumes other classes and groups, not counted here, will meet Sunday evenings or during the week. Only then can the church expect up to 200 in Sunday school attendance for every minister. To count youth, women's Bible study, and prayer groups as additional Sunday school classes will negate the accuracy of Myers's ratio. The (1 + 1): 200 ratio takes full effect only when additional groups are aiding the growth.

It is always possible to find exceptions to the rule, but since most churches are not exceptional in greatly exceeding the ratio, it will help to follow the recommended guideline. I tried out Myers's ratio in four churches. Their ratios came out (1 + 1):274, (1 + 1):198, (1 + 1):153, and (1 + 1):83. Myers's estimate was

confirmed in three of the four cases; the fourth church
needed more lay ministers devoted to reaching those
outside its membership. Many other churches can identify with this shortage of volunteer leaders.

GROWTH–INDUCING LAY MINISTERS

God uses all his people, however, not just the paid
professionals. The crucial question is, What kind of lay
ministers produce growth? In their book, *How to Grow
a Church,* Donald McGavran and Win Arn describe the
various kinds of church leaders. They discuss five
classes of leaders found in most churches. Here is a
summary.[1]

Class 1: Unpaid volunteers who serve the existing church
attenders, including Sunday school teachers,
committee members, trustees, deacons, ushers,
choir members, elders, and visitors to the sick.

Class 2: Unpaid volunteers who focus their attention on
serving and winning people not now attending
church on a regular basis. They serve as evangelistic Bible study members in homes, visitors to
newcomers to the church or community, leaders
in social services of a dozen varieties, and those
who offer a personal invitation to church or a
Christian activity.

Class 3: Unpaid or partially paid leaders of small
churches, usually in an effort to get them started
and established.

Class 4: Paid pastors and staff members who serve
churches on a full-time basis.

Class 5: Paid denominational leaders, district superinten-
dents, and missionaries to other cultures who
work outside the local church.

For the expansion of your local church class 2 leaders provide the cutting edge for reaching the uncommitted. These volunteers invite newcomers and visit first-timers to your church. They serve with love and compassion in your community in an effort to bring others to Christ. They witness aggressively and include interested unbelievers in their Christian activities. Their contact with people outside the church influences some to expose themselves to the gospel and to turn to Christ, but such effectiveness does not happen by accident. Only by exerting time, money, and energy does their commitment take on flesh and blood.

The importance of class 2 leaders in my own church struck me afresh not long ago. I asked an adult group to share how each came to know Christ as Lord and Savior. Again and again they mentioned Tuesday night visits from class 2 leaders. Their willingness to care about a newcomer with whom they previously were unacquainted made a positive impression. Although presenting the gospel with clarity, the visitors from the church avoided a high-pressure approach. A number of adults reported that they thought over their decision for a few days or even weeks before receiving Christ. Many other factors influenced their commitment, but what they remembered was the personal concern of class 2 leaders.

Think about the following questions concerning your church. How many class 2 leaders function on a regular basis? How much time, energy, and money goes into attracting new people? How many hours a week do they give as Christ's witnesses? List all the volunteer hours that people spend as class 1 workers in a month's time. In an opposite column add up the hours people from your church spend as class 2 leaders.

Brace yourself for a couple of shocks. At first glance, the number of hours the people of your church give to serving Christ will overwhelm you with gratitude. Without the labor of love by God's people, our churches and communities would sink into utter misery. Pause for a refreshing moment of thanks and praise God for the workers who sacrifice their time and energy so unselfishly. A second look will disturb you. Ponder how much of the total time goes for the church's maintenance ministry. By comparison how few hours are spent touching and telling those outside the church about Jesus Christ. Most churches fail in fulfilling the Great Commission for this crucial reason. Fifty times as many hours go into serving the saints as into evangelizing the neighborhood.

Once you sense the urgency of more effort in serving and reaching nonmembers for Christ, a logical question follows: Where can your church find more class 2 leaders? Growing churches most often enlist these all-important servants of Christ among three groups of lay people. First, new Christians with natural ties to unregenerate people provide a rich source of class 2 workers. Bob and Kendra came to know Christ in a refreshing personal experience of faith. As young Christians they felt a bubbling excitement about Jesus and the life-changing message of the gospel; yet most of their neighbors, friends, and relatives never attended church. They looked upon Bob and Kendra as "Jesus freaks."

Somehow the subject of religion kept coming up

around them. At parties, on the job, and in neighborhood conversations Bob and Kendra exuded the excitement and happiness of new life in Christ. Some of their friends thought they were slightly crazy. A few relatives took offense at their outspoken exuberance. Most, however, respected their newfound convictions and overflowing joy. During the next two years Bob and Kendra brought several neighbors and friends into the church. They too found Christ or renewed commitments from days past. Their friendship bridges served as natural paths for the good news of Christ.

Second, Christians with the spiritual gift of evangelism become class 2 leaders quite naturally. Cathy is a living illustration. According to her husband, Phil, Cathy's feet get itchy whenever too much time passes without witnessing to an unbeliever about Christ. She finds little satisfaction in life without sharing the good news often. Among the list of spiritual gifts in Ephesians 4, those with the gift of evangelism hold special importance for church growth. A small percentage of lay people using the evangelism gift with excellence will transform your church. From the wellspring of their ministries will flow a steady stream of new converts into your fellowship.

Third, the company of the committed who spend time and energy becoming effective in their role as witnesses will function as class 2 workers. In most cases effectiveness requires on-the-job training under the supervision of an experienced witness. Methods vary, but the apprenticeship pattern remains constant. Without such careful direction, many committed disciples bumble the job. Before long they make an embarrassed retreat into more comfortable class 1 service such as passing the offering plate in worship or providing cookies for a social. With personal tutoring and an adequate example, however, many lay evangelists become productive. Competence comes only with thoroughness of training and years of experience.

Quickly review the three sources for class 2 leaders —new converts, Christians with a gift for evangelism, and the committed who will give themselves to a growth-producing activity. Of the three, the last is crucial, especially for the beginning. Although these first volunteers may sense no special gifts for outreach, God will honor their concern and willingness. The Lord knows how difficult the task seems to most church members. Even the thought of their approaching the door of a stranger who visited church last Sunday, meeting that person for the first time and talking about anything—not to mention the church or Jesus—scares them out of their wits. Even a small number of committed people, however, can make a big difference in effective evangelism. It will require their best efforts for at least a year. Then they can expect to stimulate other lay evangelists and new Christians to join them.

The second vital question is what roles and gifts fit lay ministers for their task? The transformation of a person from unchurched to responsible discipleship involves three stages. In stage one, the unchurched person comes into contact with influential Christians. In this *exposure stage,* a person accepts another's invitation to attend church or a Christian activity. In stage two, the *commitment stage,* the unchurched person hears and accepts the gospel of Jesus Christ. In stage three, he feels himself a responsible part of the Christian fellowship. In most instances the person indicates a desire to enter this *discipleship stage* by joining the church.

Growth-producing people will develop ministries designed to help others through the three stages. Not every person fits each task, because personalities and spiritual gifts differ. Three specific roles keep the energy of spiritual gifts focused on church growth. *Recruiters* influence unchurched people in the exposure stage. *Evangelists* help unbelievers understand and accept the gospel in the commitment stage. *Disciplers* lead new Christians into the fellowship of the church in the discipleship stage. Pastors and church leaders will want to equip their members in each growth-producing role.

THE ROLE OF RECRUITER

Recruiters bring non-Christians into meaningful contact with Christians in your church. They recruit the unchurched for a fellowship, study, or worship activity. The people and the message expose the unregenerate person to the love of Christ. Judy, a quiet but friendly woman, lived in a neighborhood full of young mothers. As a recruiter she exposed her friends to the gospel in an attractive way. Although her approach might vary from one you might choose, the method fit her kind of neighborhood.

Judy loved the Lord and wanted her friends to know him too. She wanted to start a Bible study in her home but did not feel qualified to teach it. Through prayer and effort she found a teacher and opened her home to her friends. A half-dozen or more of her neighbors came the first day. Others joined them in the following weeks. Some women deepened their existing faith while others came to know Christ in a new and personal way. The enthusiasm of Judy and her Christian friends led several families into more active involvement in their own churches. Not surprisingly, some of the un-committed with no church home wanted to try Judy's church first.

Recruiters need help from their churches in provid-ing attractive ministries. They do not function well in isolation. What helps most is excellence with excite-ment. Recruiters thrive in a church that stimulates and fulfills its members. Thrilled with the high caliber of their church life, they cannot keep silent. No other publicity beats word of mouth recommendations from satisfied customers. With a high degree of enthusiasm for one or more Christian activities, recruiters will in-vite their friends readily.

The apostle Andrew is a biblical model of an enthusi-astic recruiter. Every time we meet him in the Fourth Gospel, he is bringing someone to Jesus. I picture An-drew as looking at you with a smile and a twinkle in his eyes. Something about him strikes you as likeable, ap-proachable, agreeable. After his first encounter with Jesus, Andrew found his brother Simon Peter (see John 1:40–42). With no doubt, no indecision, no question mark, he exclaimed, "We have found the Messiah!" He wasted no time in bringing him to Jesus. Like Andrew, recruiters begin with family and relatives where rela-tionship bridges already exist.

The next time we meet Andrew in John's Gospel he

is bringing a boy to Jesus (John 6:8–9). With the boy's lunch Jesus performed a remarkable miracle. All four Gospels tell of the five thousand who were fed from the five loaves and two fish; yet it started with a boy recruited by Andrew. Many persons can become recruiters of children. What parent or teacher knows who he may be teaching? Will one of these little ones grow into the man or woman God uses for his marvelous works in the next generation?

The final time we find Andrew in John's Gospel he is bringing some Greeks to Jesus (see John 12:20–22). The event is of pivotal importance. The Gentile world was now looking to Jesus for the answers to salvation and life. Jesus responded by looking to the cross, where he would give himself as a sacrifice. Andrew is a prototype for recruiters today. Once he discovered Jesus, he refused to keep the friendship to himself. He made it his way of life to introduce others to his best friend.

People with another kind of talent often become recruiters. They have deep commitment, a great vision, and specific skills. They may use their abilities to take pictures or write news stories about church activities for the local newspaper. They may design advertising or saturation mailings to communicate the church's welcome to newcomers. They may develop musical events that attract the unchurched. They may organize special programs with well-known speakers who will appeal to those who seldom if ever attend. Their role as recruiters become evident as the formerly untouched people find themselves exposed to Christ.

You can discover recruiters most often among people with a certain type of spiritual gift. Think about the

gifts that by their nature function best between individuals. Service, helps, mercy, exhortation, faith, and
leadership are spiritual gifts that work well in one-
on-one relationships. The function of the gift builds a
friendship bridge for effective recruiting. Regardless of
one's gifts, however, almost anyone can be encouraged
to exercise the role of inviting an unchurched relative,
neighbor, or friend to a Christian activity.

Few people become disciples of Jesus Christ and responsible members of the church without someone recruiting them. Without the Andrews inviting others to
Jesus and his message, no one can predict success in
church growth. Why not set a measurable goal of ten
percent of your congregation to join Operation Andrew as recruiters? By Operation Andrew I do not
mean a program, but a way of life. These volunteers
will give themselves to bringing others to church or a
Christian activity. Many will start with relatives and
close friends; others will concentrate on children. A few
will enjoy a wide sphere of relationships that will bring
many under the influence of Christ's good news.

THE ROLE OF EVANGELIST

A growing church cannot do without the Andrews;
but if only the recruiters function, a congregation risks
building a religious club instead of the body of Christ.
For the church to be really Christian, the role of evangelist is indispensable. Without the work of evangelism
the church of Jesus Christ will pass into extinction in a
single generation. Evangelists share the gospel in
meaningful terms and lead others to receive Jesus

Christ as Lord and Savior. Some people gasp at the thought of becoming a volunteer evangelist in the context of their own vocation, yet more and more Christians are doing it today. The trend is moving with amazing speed toward speaking up as a witness for Jesus Christ.

What are the marks of a person with unusual potential for lay evangelism? Since no one has the answer all packaged and ready to market, a biblical example will prove helpful. Philip, who is called the deacon early in the Book of Acts, later bears the title "the evangelist" (Acts 21:8). Although he has the same name as Philip the apostle, his training and experience differ vastly. We might call the apostle a professional minister, since he completed three years of training with Jesus. By the same standard we must classify Philip the deacon as a layman. He is as a biblical prototype for lay evangelists today.

In the New Testament Philip is pictured as a responsible, wise, Spirit-filled person; yet three characteristics mark him as a lay evangelist. First, Philip had *sensitivity.* He related well to people in large numbers (see Acts 8). As Philip preached, scores of Samaritans turned to Christ. Then he sensed God's direction to leave the sizable crowds and present the gospel to a lone government official. It is obvious that the official, an Ethiopian eunuch, was highly receptive. Open and ready to hear new truth from the Scriptures, he welcomed Philip's overture of friendship. The evangelist's sensitivity to him, and to the Holy Spirit, led to a redemptive connection.

Second, Philip had *fervency of conviction.* The gos-

pel burned in Philip's soul with a holy passion. With
gripping intensity he felt the urgency of proclaiming
Christ's salvation as the only answer to human lostness.
Everywhere he went, he called men and woman to
Jesus Christ as Lord and Savior. To him nothing was
more important than a person's initial saving encounter
with the risen Lord. The cliché "fiery evangelist" fits
him, not as the caricature of a shouting preacher threatening sinners with hellfire and brimstone, but as one
whose ardent feelings accompanied a sure and certain
truth that he could not keep to himself.

Finally, Philip was *persuasive.* His convincing spirit
was evident among large crowds in Samaria and with
one man on a desert road. People were impressed
when he spoke. He won over his audience, not to himself, but to his Lord; yet nothing impresses me more
about Philip's persuasive powers than what happened
in his own home. His four daughters followed his example in speaking up for Christ, and they exercised their
gifts of prophecy (see Acts 21:8–9). I know of no greater
compliment to a man's character than that his own
children follow him in the things of God.

Why not set a goal of 10 percent of your church members to join Operation Philip? Again I refer to a committed way of life, not a particular method. Churches
with rapid growth rates involve a small percentage of
lay evangelists in an organized week-by-week effort.
Often an instruction period aids these people in developing their presentation of the gospel in articulate
terms. They also receive guidance in developing their
life story of receiving Christ. The experience of growing churches shows that trained lay evangelists do more

spontaneous witnessing than others. Their training gives them more confidence and a wealth of practical experience for the unexpected moment of opportunity.

THE ROLE OF DISCIPLER

I doubt that your church will experience continuous growth without lay recruiters and evangelists; yet activating these two roles alone has led to a frustrating experience for hundreds of churches. Dozens of people indicated a decision for Christ through an active witnessing program; yet a high percentage failed to become responsible disciples. Some people refer to the problem as the "follow-up gap." To bridge the gap requires concerned Christians who will take a personal interest in new believers. Their role can help those who make an initial decision for Christ develop into responsible members in the church and active disciples of the Lord Jesus.

Disciplers love new people into the fellowship. They make newcomers to any class or group in the church feel welcome. They sense the importance of getting acquainted, helping others build friendships, and leading them into the basics of Christian living. They show interest in new Christians until they feel they belong to Christ and to a specific group within the church. God minted the coin of discipling with two sides: one is social, the other theological. On the social side, new Christians must feel a part of the church's fabric of relationships. Otherwise they will become irregular in worship and study and drift away to another church or drop out entirely.

Social acceptance alone, however, does not make a disciple of Jesus Christ. On the theological side, disciplers help the new Christians develop disciplines that will spur them toward maturity. Part of the growing commitment will be the procedures for becoming full members of the church. Without undue pressure, growing churches constantly offer the opportunity for church membership. I must, however, speak up about the danger of altering biblical requirements for membership. More than one church has destroyed its future effectiveness by accepting members who did not meet the biblical criteria. A call for balance is imperative so that membership standards will neither include unbelievers nor exclude immature Christians.

My favorite example of a discipler in the Bible is Barnabas. William Barclay, a popular Scottish scholar, calls him ". . . the man with the biggest heart in the church."[2] Certain characteristics in his life set a pattern for disciplers in all ages. Barnabas *always believed the best* about a fellow Christian, even one as suspicious as Saul of Tarsus. When Saul claimed Jesus Christ had turned him around, the disciples in Jerusalem refused to believe it, or accept him. They gave him the cold shoulder. You can understand their feelings.

The Jerusalem disciples thought Saul had joined the spy business. They suspected their arch-persecutor of adopting a deceitful ploy. By becoming an undercover agent in Christian guise, he would discover the followers of the Way. They feared he would send them to prison or to death, but Barnabas believed the best about Saul. Taking him to the leaders of the Jerusalem church, Barnabas vouched for his conversion. He documented the validity of Saul's transformation by reporting his public preaching of Christ in Damascus. Because the apostles knew Barnabas and trusted him, they accepted Saul.

Another quality of Barnabas' ministry is worthy of imitation by every discipler. He felt *every Christian deserved a second chance.* His nephew, John Mark, was on the team of the first missionary expedition with Barnabas and Saul. He started with high expectations, but along the way he deserted. The Bible gives no hint about why he returned home. At the time, Barnabas refused to support Mark's action. He stuck by Saul and completed the journey. Some years later at the Jerusalem council, Barnabas came into contact with his nephew again. Convinced that he would prove reliable now, Barnabas wanted to give him a second chance on the next missionary journey.

Saul, by then known as Paul, disagreed. He preferred to "go with the winners" and bypass the unpredictable kind. A "sharp clash of opinion" (Acts 15:39, PHILLIPS) followed. (It is of some comfort to know that gifted apostles also had feet of clay.) Barnabas stuck by his intention to help Mark, no matter what the consequences. Paul proved implacable as well. The two missionary pioneers therefore divided their proposed route and set out on separate trips. In God's providence two missionary teams were proclaiming the gospel and planting churches instead of one.

A final characteristic of Barnabas was that he *helped others discover their God-given ministry* without feeling threatened by their success or leadership qualities. One might wonder how Paul, had it not been for God's

using Barnabas, might have become the great missionary. Paul's church-building ministry throughout his
fruitful journeys revealed the influence of Barnabas.
Paul mentions his former colleague several times in the
Epistles, always with utmost respect. One might also
wonder if Mark ever would have written the Gospel by
his name, or become Peter's associate, or later Paul's.
The fruit of Barnabas' ministry was in the lives of others.

To spot disciplers in your church, keep alert to a
special type of spiritual gift. Pay special attention to
teaching, preaching, administration, and hospitality.
These gifts find expression in a *group* of people. As a
result, their function encourages a discipler role. It requires special concern, however, for the discipler to
give extra attention to the newcomer. Otherwise the
benefit of ministry will not reach beyond the existing
fellowship. What marks off disciplers from other lay
leaders is their helpfulness to new Christians.

Dave and Brenda became leaders in a new Sunday
school class for couples in their twenties. They let others teach while they gave themselves to developing the
fellowship life of the group. The couple started a home
Bible study, worked with officers in planning monthly
socials, and constantly invited class members to their
home. They made every effort to build the class's
morale and welcome new people. Others in the group
were filling the roles of recruiters and evangelists. Dave
and Brenda participated in these efforts but found their
greatest effectiveness as disciplers. Under their leadership the class began to grow in spiritual maturity and
in numbers, first doubling and then tripling within a
couple of years.

Why not set a measurable goal of ten percent of your congregation to join Operation Barnabas as disciplers? Begin with the people who already function like Barnabas; then encourage others to join their ranks. They will emerge as you add more face-to-face groups in Sunday school and church. Additional groups will enable more "places of welcome" in which newcomers will find a home. Of special importance is a class for young Christians on the basics of belief and practice. Often an elective class of only a few weeks duration, but repeated often, will make a significant contribution.

SPIRITUAL MOTIVATION FOR LAY MINISTERS

Who would refuse more Andrews, Philips, and Barnabases in their fellowship? How does a church find more of these vital workers? *What will motivate lay ministers to reach others for Christ and the church?* I do not pretend to answer fully, but let me offer a few suggestions that have worked well in some churches. First, lay ministers need the inner conviction that "this is what God wants me to do." From the depths of their beings lay leaders must believe *God* wants them to touch non-Christians redemptively. The inner call of his direction comes upon new workers when God's people really pray (see Matthew 9:38, Luke 10:2).

A wholesome desire for God's best leads to a satisfying joy in serving the Lord. Pastor C. W. Perry sets a wise example by urging, "Ask God what he wants you to do." For the Christian in right relationship with the Lord, the simple prayer "What shall I do, Lord?" (Acts 22:10, RSV) can be life changing. It lifts motivation from psychological manipulation to a high spiritual plane. People who are witnessing and working only because of someone's harassment will soon tire of it. Maybe you observed the extreme form in your own church near the beginning of some school year. Do you recall the new person who arrived on the scene with fresh vigor and eager enthusiasm? He had a problem saying no; so well-meaning church members talked him into taking ten jobs in the next two months. By Lent you held his funeral. He died of sheer exhaustion.

When it comes to inner motivation, what people tell themselves makes a gigantic difference. With the conviction that "Christ wants me to touch other lives" comes a special excitement in witnessing. The Lord himself gives a feeling of self-esteem, worth, and importance, but a complaining spirit destroys the joy of the Lord. Murmuring "I'm killing myself with church activities" produces fatigue and exhaustion. How much better are the God-motivated witnesses who count their labor as joy. Musing "I'm serving the Lord because he wants me to" gives energy and ambition.

Second, lay ministers will most often follow the personal example set by the pastor, staff members, and lay "opinion makers." As the leaders go, so goes the church. Growth will seldom happen without the full support of the pastor. More than anyone else, he sets the philosophy and direction of the congregation. The pastor's own life-style in evangelism and discipleship will be caught more than taught. Either the pastor or another staff member must invest a major portion of time and energy in effective evangelism. Most churches do not grow because they commit so little prayer, thought, time, energy, money, and credit sharing to the task of church growth.

Pastors face a continual challenge to manage their time for maximum benefit. In the majority of churches with a single pastor, I recommend that one day a week be devoted to the most productive activities for church growth. In larger churches one staff person needs to use 60 percent or more of his time in growth efforts. Good stewardship calls for concentrating energies on what produces the most growth. Sunday school provides excellent growth for many churches. On-the-job training for lay evangelists proves effective for others. Home Bible studies produce converts for many. Why not make a hard-thinking evaluation of results?

It is high time to concentrate on what yields healthy growth and to abandon nonproductive programs, but a word of caution is necessary. Wisdom calls for discovering a better way first. Find a growth-producing method that works in your situation *before* dropping other activities. Too many church leaders find it easier to chop with the axe than to build with hammer and nails. A personal example of effective evangelism backed by a sizeable time-energy commitment from the pastor remains irreplaceable. It motivates lay ministers as nothing else will. When words and deeds focus together on a single objective, influence follows.

Third, lay ministers will flounder without the personal conviction of the importance of their church-growth ministry. Where do they find such assurance? Most will not believe their task is all important unless their pastor and "significant others" keep telling them so. "Significant others" include the unpaid lay leaders who are opinion-makers in the church. With their full approval lay recruiters, evangelists, and disciplers can flourish. Without their heartfelt blessing, few class 2 leaders will emerge in strength and power. The communication of enthusiastic endorsement from such leaders helps immensely.

It takes something special to keep church growth high on the priority list. For those with the spiritual gift of evangelism, the feeling of first importance will bubble up from the effervescence of the Holy Spirit. For others, it requires careful discernment matched with balanced insight into the Scriptures. For all Christians, the matter of bearing witness to others calls for a constant gaze at Jesus Christ. Only in sharing his heart and compassion do the company of the committed absorb God's yearning love for the lost; yet without constant care wrong attitudes will undermine the priority of effective evangelism. Other concerns, often legitimate in their proper place, will crowd out the essential respect for the lay minister of church growth.

In subtle ways people give a sense of distinction to those engaging in tasks they believe most vital. Why do medical doctors receive more pay than college professors? The demands of education and discipline are about the same, but most people believe physical health is more important than advanced education. Consequently, they reward physicians, not only with money, but also with considerable esteem and social status. Many local congregations operate the same way. Churches with a youth director or minister of education abound; yet in many denominations a minister of evangelism–church growth is a rare bird. It is encouraging to report, however, that this uncommon species is on the increase.

Every church holds a hidden agenda of priorities. It spends its time, energy, and money accordingly, and the annual treasurer's report often mirrors a congregation's real values. What is shocking is how low on the scale of actual expenditures church growth rates. Even churches who say they give special attention to outreach often neglect it financially. Growing churches spend sizable sums of money for the single task of winning the unregenerate. In addition they manage other expenditures in a way that will help rather than hinder growth. When church growth ministries are really important in a church, it will show up in its budget.

Fourth, successful experience in recruiting, evangelizing, or discipling adds motivation. All Christians thrill to the touch of the Holy Spirit in using them to reach others. The fun of fishing is in the catching. Fishers of men need not come home empty-handed in our desperate times of emptiness, loneliness, and alienation. Nothing will confirm one's spiritual gifts quite like positive results in the lives of others. Lasting satisfaction results as lay ministers observe new Christians progress toward spiritual maturity. A valid sense of accomplishment stimulates greater efforts.

Fifth, lay ministers respond to recognition and appreciation for what they are doing. Heartfelt praise and a genuine word of thanks give new hope to flagging spirits. When it comes from an admired pastor or respected leader, it holds special significance. A letter, a note, or even a postcard will add motivation to a faithful worker. A private word of commendation or passing along another's compliment will help even more. Your caring reminds the recruiter, evangelist, or discipler that God remembers too. Encouragement gives new heart to a tired body.

A quick review of this chapter will reinforce answers to three crucial questions: (1) What kind of lay ministers produce growth? (2) What roles and gifts fit them for their task? (3) What will motivate lay ministers to reach others for Christ and the church? Discovering your role in church growth gives focus and direction to your personal ministry. The startling self-revelation that "I can do it" may lead you to develop your church-growth ministry with fresh vigor; yet unless the Lord crowns your efforts with success, a sense of frustration sets in. It makes sense therefore to concentrate your energy and resources on the people who are most receptive. The last chapter will help you find them. Next, however, it will pay high dividends to learn how to retain more of a church's present members.

NOTES

1. Donald A. McGavran and Win C. Arn, *How to Grow a Church* (Glendale, Cal.: Regal Books, 1973), pp. 89–97.
2. William Barclay, *The Acts of the Apostles,* The Daily Study Bible Series (Philadelphia: Westminster Press, 1955), p. 95.

4. Close the Back Door

"Christians are Christ's body, the organism through which He works. Every addition to that body enables Him to do more."

—C. S. LEWIS

In today's open climate, many churches are leading people to initial decisions for Christ.* Most professions of faith appear sincere and wholehearted; yet a cry of anguish rises from frustrated church leaders. "New people come in the front door and a short time later they slip out the back." What is the problem? What is the solution? Some church leaders point the finger and in an accusing tone ask, "Who left the back door open?" One will blame the pastor with the complaint, "We are simply not getting fed." Another will criticize fellow church members for their lethargy and low commitment.

The pastor often suspects a spiritual disease. He feels that one or two families take pleasure in thwarting his best efforts; so he calls for spiritual renewal or outright confession of sin. Meanwhile the decision makers on the governing body of the church grieve over the back-

---

* Portions of this chapter originally appeared in Charles Mylander, "Your Church Needs a Multiple Staff," *Christianity Today,* 24 March 1978, © 1978 by *Christianity Today,* and are reprinted by permission.

door problem. Although they like their pastor as a person and a friend, they question his leadership ability. They wonder if it is about time for him to change churches. In many instances, however, the real problem remains undiscovered.

Tragic! Most church leaders seldom see the cause, not to mention the cure, of the open back door. If an acceptable quality of leadership, a reasonable degree of spiritual health, and a functioning system of evangelism exist, then the cause of the back-door problem may well be "sociological strangulation." Any one of a number of sociological factors may stifle the church's growth. Too few parking spaces, too few classes, or too few staff members can do it. *Sociological factors do not cause growth, but they can thwart it.* Any growth-restricting obstacle can hinder the grace of God.

Any class or group will reach a maximum size beyond which it will not grow. When the attendance reaches its "full" level, "closure" sets in. The group closes off to any significant expansion. It happens whenever the number of dropouts matches the new attenders. It's like a bathtub half full of cold, dirty water. If a little child turns on the hot water to full pressure and then skips out to the back yard with the rest of the family, water will soon flood the house. The bathtub, however, still holds only its original capacity.

Inside the bathtub the quality changed from dirty to clean and from cold to hot, but the quantity remained only one tub "full." In the same way, sociological factors limit the average attendance potential of a class or group to a "full" level. Excellent teaching and warm relationships may improve the quality. Evangelistic efforts may transform some present members and add fervent new Christians. For each new person who becomes active, however, a member on the edge of the group becomes inactive. A church can prevent its growth through the sociological sin of "closure."

The closure principle leads to the discovery of an important secret. If a church's number of classes and groups remains the same, it will level off in attendance. A church's classes and groups are similar to a house with only so many comfortable places to sit. On a special anniversary reception more friends arrive than the couches and chairs can accommodate. Whenever some guests leave the room to visit with friends or refill their coffee cups, others make themselves comfortable in the vacated spaces. When those who left the room for a moment return, they find no place to sit. Somehow they no longer feel as if they belong. With few noticing, some begin to slip out the door.

This chapter will focus on structures and relationships that fortify a sense of belonging. It will suggest three ways to close the back door. *First, a balanced increase in "circles of commitment" will help a church retain more members. Second, a multiple staff with loving relationships will help solve the problem.* Satisfying staff relationships create an atmosphere and stimulate ideas that slow down the turnover rate of members. *Third, careful observance of church-growth ratios will release the grip of sociological strangulation.* You can use the ratios to discover the strangulation points in your church, and then apply corrective action.

The best efforts to close the back door of the church will not accomplish the task completely. Theological

insights explain part of the problem. Not every pro-
fessed "convert" received Christ or the Holy Spirit's
regeneration, but many did open themselves to Christ
and experience his saving power. In their lives, the
back-door problem means the difference between
fruitful Christian living and sterile inactivity. Whatever
church leaders can do to prevent unnecessary losses
will make Christianity a more powerful force for good.
Slowing down the turnover rate will produce a substan-
tial improvement in both Christian nurture and church
growth.

CIRCLES OF COMMITMENT

To close the back door, the first step is to develop
more circles of commitment. I refer to what C. Peter
Wagner and others call the "membership circle, fellowship circles, and kinship circles."[1] The terms refer primarily to the types of group life experienced by committed Christians rather than to programs or
organizations. In church-growth terminology the membership circle functions as a *celebration* in corporate
worship. *Celebration* is not the best word to describe
the membership circle, but since it has already been
introduced into discussions of church growth, it is probably wise to retain it. The fellowship circles associate as
congregations, or large groups within the church. The
kinship circles operate as *cells,* or small groups of a
hundred varieties.

A healthy church worships together in celebration
and adds congregations and multiple cells. Worship services alone will not keep a church growing. The wor-

ship celebration needs the fellowship support of multiple congregations or else its growth will cease. Congregations in turn thrive on an increasing number of cells, but cells fail to generate lasting power without an organic tie to a vital congregation. For maximum benefit, church leaders will consciously develop all three circles of commitment.

The church as celebration worships God with expectancy and joy. Any Christian can worship alone in the beauty of the woods or the majesty of the mountains, but the private experience of worship will never replace the public celebration of God's presence. Celebration radiates a festive mood that results only from a great gathering of like-minded worshipers. Faith and fervency charge the atmosphere. The climate created by joyful singing, moving silence, or inspiring preaching contributes to the sense of the Spirit's presence. A spiritual celebration remains a personal matter, yet possible only in concert with other people gathered for corporate worship.

In normal usage the words *church* and *congregation* are interchangeable synonyms. In preceding chapters I have so used them, but more precise definitions are now necessary. The word *church* will now refer to the total membership of a local assembly. *Congregation,* however, will mean a fellowship circle within the church. With 200 or fewer in worship, a church may have only one congregation. The membership circle and the fellowship circle remain one and the same, but as a church grows, it will sooner or later have multiple congregations within it.

Few churches will grow beyond 250 in average worship attendance without congregational groupings. Large Sunday school classes, choirs, and sizable women's groups are the most common congregations. In large churches congregations may form around athletics, bus ministries, sizable Bible studies, and other activities. Adding congregations allows a growing church to expand and yet keep the personal touch. A member can miss the worship celebration for several Sundays, and few will notice; but if he misses the congregation for two or three weeks, friends will know at once!

"Where were you? Out of town?"

"Are your kids sick?"

"What's going on? We haven't seen you much lately."

What are the marks of a distinct congregation within a church? The participants know one another's names and feel a sense of mutual loyalty. They hold one another accountable for attendance and somehow communicate a personal message to absentees. In their own way they say, "We care about you. We missed you." Although congregations provide good instruction, meaningful service, and enjoyable social activities, they seldom specialize in spiritual intimacy. The closer relationship, aptly called a *kinship circle,* requires a cell.

Kinship suggests family and close relatives. Like families, cells have distinguishing marks. A close-knit bond of love, an open communication about Christian experiences, and an honest accountability in spiritual matters give evidence of a genuine cell. Commitment to life in Christ is both personal and sharable. Typical activities of a cell include sharing personal problems, praying for one another, discussing the Bible, enjoying spiritual friendships, and serving people outside the kinship circle. The Christian who desires maximum development will participate in all three—a worship celebration, a congregation, and a cell. What's more, many congregations will increase their growth rate by multiplying effective cell groups.

The relationship between the number of cells and effective evangelism is greater than is often expected. The religious sociologist Richard A. Myers conducted a year-long experiment with cooperating churches.[2] He asked all the participants to keep close tabs on attendance and church membership. Then he divided their pastors into two groups and issued near-opposite instructions. He asked one group to combine Sunday school classes whenever a teacher resigned. He requested that they merge the students into another class their own age and make it larger. He instructed the other group of ministers to increase the number of classes. They were to divide the students for an additional class of equal enrollment in each children's department. They were also to recruit additional teachers for each of the new classes.

At the close of the designated year the two groups of pastors compared results. The contrast was astonishing. Those who combined classes returned discouraged and disheartened. Their larger classes, resulting from merging groups when a teacher resigned, dwindled in attendance. In fact, by year's end membership in most combined classes had declined. The average attendance was about the same as only one of the classes before the merger. Worse yet, the ministers not only reported decreased Sunday school attendance but also a decline in church membership.

The pastors who added teachers and divided

classes returned with glowing reports. Each of their
divided classes grew until they regained their previous size. The new classes expanded too. In addition
to the increased Sunday school attendance, the ministers also reported gains in church membership. The
application seems obvious. The first set of pastors in-
hibited the growth of their classes and opened the
back doors of their churches. The second set gave
more opportunities for good learning and meaningful relationships. They built more "bathtubs," and
their churches grew.

Numerous church leaders do not realize how many
cells operate in their churches already. Sunday school
classes of a dozen students or less serve as cells. Some
committees work like cells. Visitation teams, club programs, small musical groups, Bible studies, athletic
teams, and a host of other activities encourage the close
relationships of a kinship circle. Furthermore, many
cells function as spontaneous friendships without any
organizational bond. As friends, the committed encourage one another often and hold one another accountable for Christian living. Eliminate the cell life from
almost any church, and it will soon die.

One significant secret of church growth is to multiply
cells and expand kinship circles. Most churches grow
through building relationships. The lonely need them,
the friendly want them, those with special interests
seek them. The discerning church will concentrate on
multiplying the kinds of cells God is blessing in their
present ministry. If the Lord is honoring the Sunday
school, then add more Sunday school classes. If the Holy
Spirit is using sports activities for outreach and a sense

of belonging, then multiply various athletic groups. New kinds of kinship circles will emerge as the demand warrants.

The principle of multiplying cells for growth is so important that it will merit further discussion later in this chapter. The church-growth ratios will then be more precise in how many to launch in relationship to workers. The principle of multiplying cells within a congregation also applies to adding congregations within a church, or adding churches to a denomination. New circles of commitment enable growth; mergers result in decline. Given the proper leadership, more circles of commitment attract more people, but few emerge automatically. Marshaling personal concern and mobilizing qualified workers remain essential for multiplying cells and congregations.

The close of chapter 3 concerned principles for mobilizing more workers for recruiting, evangelizing, and discipling. The same guidelines apply to enlisting leaders for congregations and cells. At the crucial point of engaging workers, powerful prayer will make a vast difference. Without prayer, the turnover rate of new recruits will run high. From intense intercession will flow volunteers marked by added stability and increased quality. Jesus himself instructed the disciples to implore the Lord of the harvest to send out laborers (see Matthew 9:37–38, Luke 10:2). The responsibility to pray earnestly for new workers in the Lord's harvest falls on every Christian.

MULTIPLE STAFF ON LIMITED FINANCES

Although all must pray, church staff members hold special responsibility for multiplying volunteer workers. My conviction is that every church, no matter how tiny, needs a multiple staff. No church can expect sustained growth if one pastor does all the work. Jesus practiced a multiple-staff approach with the apostles. Paul employed it with his team of missionaries. Somehow, however, in later history a "one pastor, one church" syndrome set in. Fortunately, this unbiblical pattern is beginning to change. Growing churches today are recovering a multiple-staff mentality.

Any discussion of adding staff members raises the question of finances. With an all-too-tight budget at present, how can a church even consider adding a staff person? Some churches are doing it, and others can learn their secrets. Churches with a healthy growth pattern take an enlightened step of faith. Their experience shows that a capable staff member will result in more tithing families. In two years the additional income will underwrite his salary and the expanded program to go with the growth; so the church leaders trust the Lord and challenge their people to provide the finances for the initial salary.

Please wave a warning flag in front of nongrowing churches who want to hire a staff member. Churches without a healthy growth pattern often find such an act presumptuous. They may add a staff person only to discover other hindrances to growth. Their real problem may be lack of lay leaders engaged in evangelism and discipleship. Or they may suffer from too few Sunday school teachers. Or disunity within the fellowship may absorb the energy intended to help a congregation get outside itself. Then frustrations multiply, and financial difficulties follow.

Almost any church, whether growing or not, can add growth-producing staff people without placing itself in financial jeopardy. The secret is to engage a "lay minister of _____" or a "director of _____" who serves on an unpaid basis. More and more churches are reaping benefits from unpaid lay leaders with a special responsibility. Many church leaders can expect a pleasant surprise by developing this already-proven idea. The number of productive hours donated by volunteers with a recognized commission, personal office, expense account, and significant responsibility will shock many skeptics. Consider two examples.

A church in California enlists lay volunteers as staff members with sizable responsibilities and no pay. In time their ministry develops until they are working half time. When the number of hours becomes overwhelming, the church gives them a modest part-time salary. If the task becomes large enough, and cannot be divided into other volunteer positions, a person may work into a professional position on a full-time basis. At this writing only the founding pastor and one staff member were recruited from outside the church. A half-dozen others on the paid staff (most part time) came from within the membership.

A church in Indiana was growing well when the associate pastor resigned. The senior pastor could not immediately find a replacement; so he prayed for the names of thirty men in his church who would serve as unpaid lay pastors. As God impressed names on his mind, he appealed to the men to respond. As each one answered the call to commitment, he received a specific responsibility and full recognition by the church as a whole. The pastor then poured most of his energy into equipping these thirty men for their various pastoral duties. In the next few years the church nearly doubled in size (from 600 to 1,100). Lay participation is the key.

Almost every church already has two or three people who show special gifts in some growth-producing activity. Be aware of what it takes to make them effective. Look for evidence of special gifts. Grant appropriate titles and commissions with commensurate responsibilities. Provide offices with desks and names on the doors, even if these double as Sunday school classrooms. Furnish a generous expense account. Most important of all, the pastor must put in the time and effort to help lay staff members develop their potentials. They will succeed as he gives them priority in prayer, personal attention, and vision sharing.

The question often arises as to what kind of staff person to hire first. The answer depends on a church's growth pattern. In most churches a capable secretary is the first person to add. As first choice look for a member of your church who has the respect of the people. A church will benefit by selecting a mature person with emotional and spiritual stability. Most pastors run out of time, even for vital growth-producing activities. A good secretary will take over much of the essential paper work so that the pastor can concentrate on his areas of ministerial strength. If nongrowth is the pattern, check out the secretarial services first.

If too few are entering the front door of the church, engage a pastor of church-growth/evangelism. Look for a person with gifts to enable others to function as recruiters, evangelists, and disciplers. This pastor's vision must focus on winning new people and incorporating them into the church. If too many are slipping out the back door of the church, engage a director of Christian education or a minister of parish and family life. To slow the slippage, major responsibility of this staff person will involve adding congregations and multiplying cells. Growing churches often add a staff member in an area of present strength to maximize effectiveness. Their productive course of action reinforces the ministries that the Lord is already blessing.

A WORKING PHILOSOPHY OF STAFF RELATIONSHIPS

The key mobilizers of the company of the committed are the church staff members, paid or volunteer. The crucial task of enlisting, training, and deploying workers for various tasks depends most upon their initiative. In ripplelike circles of influence the relationships of the staff members will affect everything a church does. Their attitudes and examples set the pace for the lay leaders. As the lay leadership of the church moves, so move the people. What happens in staff relationships will sooner or later reach the outermost rim of congregational life. What about the members of your church staff—are they compatible or combatible?

Cleta almost apologized to the pastor for what hap-

pened while he was on vacation. No surprise. She was
the loyal type, the kind who for years taught Sunday
school and loved every minute of it. Cleta was reporting on the new associate pastor. "I don't want to hurt
your feelings, pastor," she began, "but Dick did a wonderful job of preaching while you were gone." The
understanding pastor slipped his arm around the el-
derly saint's shoulders. "Cleta," he smiled, "that just
shows what good judgment we have! You wouldn't expect us to hire anyone but the best, would you?"

Cleta smiled with an obvious sense of relief. Everything was all right because her pastor did not feel
threatened. It was okay for the new associate to succeed. Cleta is no fool. She simply discerns possible problems quicker than some people do. In all too many
churches, staff tensions do indeed mar the fellowship
and hinder the growth. It is no small problem.

The Sunday-front syndrome reaches its ugly tenta-
cles into the heart relationships of far too many church
staffs. Everything looks good on Sunday, but infighting
rumbles during the week. Sometimes the situation
deteriorates until the pastor gives nearly all of his creative energy to solving staff conflicts. The tragedy is that
the pastor has little time left for personal devotions,
study, and care of the members. Strange to tell, some
church members believe their pastors and staff are im-
mune from interpersonal tensions; yet they know pressures from secular job relationships touch virtually
every working person. So why should the devil and his
cohorts limit their attacks to the laity?

I feel deep satisfaction in my role as an associate
pastor; yet real temptations and subtle pressures in two

churches over an eight-year period alert me to the danger of conflict. I believe the devil's legions take diabolical delight in a struggle for power and prestige among church staff members. What is funnier, from Satan's viewpoint, than committed Christian leaders who preach love on Sunday and stab one another in the back during the week? Heart-to-heart conversations with pastors and associates uncover a bloody path of injured victims and damaged congregations. What can be done about it? Is it inevitable? Do Christian leaders know a better way?

A working philosophy of multiple-staff relationships eliminates much of the heartache and pain. Without apology, I propose the model from the church where I now serve. Its effective senior pastor, C. W. Perry, leads the way in producing an unusual harmony and loyalty among the staff. Although these guidelines may not fit every church, they will serve as an example that works. They can also help every church member to understand the need for firm principles as foundations for strong staff relationships. It makes little difference in terms of attitudes whether the staff is paid or volunteer. The same principles apply, at least in spirit, to small churches and large.

GUIDELINES FOR THE SENIOR PASTOR

The senior minister sets the tone for the whole church as well as the staff. In his God-given position, the pastor's actions and attitudes are crucial. He walks a tightrope. On one end of the balance pole hang the initiative and authority of leadership. On the other end

dangle the attitudes of tenderness, openness, and vul-
nerability. If the pastor leans too far either way, he loses
his balance and courts disaster. The following four practical guidelines are important to his role.

First, a competent senior pastor will view each associate as a colleague, not as a competitor. The hidden
pressure on a pastor's ego builds when an associate really succeeds and church members praise him openly.
In secret the pastor may wonder, "What if my associate's following becomes too large?" A senior pastor is
probably less than honest if he does not admit feeling
somewhat threatened. Consider Pastor Earl and his
young associate, Mark, for example. As a junior high
school student Mark accepted Christ under Pastor
Earl's ministry. The discerning man of God soon sensed
the Lord's gifts in the young man's life and encouraged
their development. In time, Mark not only graduated
from a nearby seminary but became a full-time youth
director in his home church.

As the church grew and needed more staff members,
Pastor Earl asked Mark to become his associate pastor.
A couple of years later the church took a giant step of
faith and started a daughter congregation. Mark was
God's man for the new church. Pastor Earl supported
him to the hilt, but later admitted his fear of losing all
the young married couples. He knew the families near
Mark's age would help launch the new congregation.
He also wondered if they would inadvertently deal a
crippling blow to the mother church. Some one hundred young adults did in fact make the move with the
full blessing of the mother church. Instead of cringing
in fear, Pastor Earl led the mother church to move out

in faith, adding staff and expanding facilities. Within a year the mother church was averaging more people in attendance than before the new congregation started.

Not every potential staff conflict winds up with a Cinderella ending. A young minister became an associate in an established church with a new senior minister. His story is that the senior pastor used him like a servant boy. He griped about the "carry my briefcase upstairs for me" type of treatment. The senior pastor could see only the new staff member's utter lack of loyalty. Soon each was criticizing the other's ministry. The associate found allies in the personnel committee who hired him. The senior pastor appealed to elders in the church. At the sad end of the squabble, both men left the church, hurt and blaming each other.

When an ever-increasing number of people appreciate the God-given ministry of an associate, the best senior pastors feel more secure. Instead of mentally developing some hidden fear, they check threatening thoughts with sound reasoning. "His success is *our* success. His effectiveness helps us accomplish the mission our Lord has given to us." Please note the *our* and *us* vocabulary on which effective team leaders thrive. *We* replaces *I.*

Second, a sensitive senior pastor will build the esteem of each staff member in everyone's eyes. Successful pastors major on credit sharing and partnership. Both in public and in private they speak of staff members with respect and appreciation. The matter of titles is an example. In more and more churches senior ministers are honoring permanent staff members as associate or minister of evangelism, Christian education, youth, and so on. They reserve the title "assistant" for temporary interns or seminary students fulfilling field-work assignments. In a dozen other ways they build respect for each associate, establishing the idea of a permanent team.

Few church members recognize the unintentional social pressure that a capable associate receives from well-meaning people. In a complimentary tone of voice, a friend will ask honestly, "When are you going to have your own church?" The associate, however, hears the not-so-subtle implication that "arriving" means occupying the senior position. A qualified associate sometimes hears another left-handed compliment indirectly: "He won't stay; he's too good." Again the feeling tone is that associates are either second rate or will become a head pastor in the near future.

The alert associate, by the way, soon learns to put friends at ease with some common sense talk. "I like it here. My ministry lets me do all the things I enjoy most and few of the tasks I dislike. I imagine you would like such a job, wouldn't you? I hope the Lord never calls me to another church!" If he really means it, a few friends will understand this point of view, but the social pressure to become "top dog" never disappears. The associate must learn to live with it.

Third, a successful senior pastor will let each staff member work in his area of strength. Pastor Schell founded a new church. God blessed his faithfulness, and the church grew. In time he began looking for an associate pastor with strength in Christian education. When Greg seemed to fit the need, the church hired him. Pastor Schell's philosophy is to fit the job to the person, not the person to the job. Once Greg was at work, the wise Pastor Schell noted where the Lord blessed his ministry for the good of the church. As their numbers kept growing, Greg received more responsibility in the kinds of ministry where he proved most profitable for the Kingdom. Some tasks, of course, required doing whether Greg found them enjoyable or not. But as most of his energy went into the kind of ministry he did best, the earned respect of the church members followed naturally.

Like good marriages, healthy staff relationships require constant attention. Alert senior pastors meet often with their staff to keep communication lines open and to develop warm friendships. The best staff meetings incorporate the proper mix of worship, prayer, fellowship, brainstorming, idea testing, planning, and reporting. In this setting each staff member's strengths become obvious to the others. Bouncing ideas off of other committed leaders gives added insights to any plan of action. Each person can avoid pitfalls and discover new possibilities. Then he can concentrate on the kinds of ministry in which he excels.

Finally, an outstanding senior pastor will stress financial generosity for the staff members. He will take the initiative in speaking up for them at the time of salary review. If the senior pastor wants to keep associates on the staff, a near-starvation wage will not do. In an inflationary economy it is all too easy for staff salaries to lag behind those of most lay persons. Every staff member needs to live on an economic par with the people of the church. A helpful guideline is to raise the associates' salaries to as close to the senior pastor's as possible.

Because it spares them the humiliation of begging for a livable income, the associates will feel deep gratitude.

GUIDELINES FOR THE ASSOCIATES

The senior pastor sets a constructive tone and helpful policies for a spirit of teamwork. If staff members want God's best for the church, they will embrace the senior minister's initiatives. A staff member who goes his own way only causes confusion and strife. A trouble-making staff member can foul up the best senior pastor in the world. For a successful team effort, each associate must practice workable principles of cooperation as well. No teamwork works without a team. In relationship to the senior pastor, consider four guidelines for a staff member.

First, an able associate will pray for the senior minister's success, not his job. Some years ago I caught myself playing with a deadly daydream. I wandered down the hall to the senior pastor's office. The door stood wide open, although he was out at the moment. Stepping inside I began to imagine myself sitting in his chair, occupying his large office, exercising his responsibilities. All at once I awakened to the jarring reality of my fantasy. "What am I doing?" I asked myself, knowing full well that it was the sinister sin of envy. It only took a moment to get back to work and seek the Lord's help in correcting my perspective.

A cooperative church staff is like a good football team. Members must play their positions well. If an individual member succeeds along with all the others, the team advances the ball. If an individual fails, the whole team loses ground. The best players, however, do more. They not only execute their own task with excellence but also rush to the aid of their teammates. Flexibility to seize the unexpected opportunity on any play is a mark of greatness.

Second, effective associates will always remember that they are assistants. They will not want to be called an assistant or treated like one, but they know, if they are perceptive, that their first job is to assist the senior pastor. Each senior minister somehow communicates the special ways he likes or expects assistance. It may mean preaching during his absence, relieving some part of the workload, or confirming his good ideas for the church's future. Helpful staff members will do their best, regardless of what personal limitations they may feel. As servants of the Lord, they will give their full support to the total church program.

A hearty lift in a time of need produces a response of genuine appreciation. Think of times when a little assistance makes a big difference. A husband may move the heaviest furniture in the house, but when moving an awkward mattress, a helping hand from his wife lightens the load immensely. While camping, a father may have the strength to carry a small log by himself. But if his strapping young son grabs hold of the other end, log carrying turns from drudgery into pleasure. So a church staff member will discover a warm response of gratitude by giving some relief to an overworked senior pastor.

Third, qualified associates will let the boss be the boss. They will not try to take over the helm of the ship or grab the wheel. Two churches that I know of went through traumatic times because someone ignored this simple principle. In one church two men shared the pastorate. They tried to cooperate and let each other major in his own strengths. Both were capable and had proven records of effectiveness. A church with two bosses, however, is a two-headed monster. Both pastors soon resigned.

The other church went through a painful split. An emotional issue caught the attention, but it was only the flag on the mountain. Beneath it lay a deeper cause of friction. Two leaders developed two different philosophies of ministry for several years. Two styles of ministry meant two followings in the same church. In spite of several title changes, neither was the leader recognized by the whole church. When the boss was not the boss, conflict was inevitable.

Every staff member needs to think through the Bible's teaching on authority, spiritual gifts, and loyalty. Spirit-filled associates should find nothing more satisfying than fulfilling the desires of the one in authority. They will discipline themselves to respond to any suggestion from the senior pastor quickly, thoroughly, and conscientiously. What will embarrass an associate most is a reminder to do something the senior pastor already requested. Efficient staff members will make "quick to respond" a living motto of their service. When they do not agree with the senior pastor's suggestion, they will pray, communicate, and work hard to resolve the differences. Maintaining unity receives high priority in the Scripture.

Finally, an outstanding associate will remain loyal when others criticize the senior minister. Most criticism contains a grain of truth, however distorted and exaggerated the facts. The temptation to lend an understanding ear is ever present. Some church members will try to manipulate a situation by communicating dissatisfactions indirectly through a staff member, but associates can avoid "being used" by insisting that the person talk to the appropriate person in charge. It is amazing how criticism fades when the people involved talk face to face. Of course, confrontation will accomplish little without attitudes of Christian love and forgiveness.

In our church a workable staff meeting rule is to use personal names. Every staff member knows better than to mention a criticism with the ambiguous, "They say. . . ." A matter too confidential to use personal names should never be discussed. Whenever anyone slips a "they say" into the conversation, the others immediately ask, "Who are 'they'?" This open and honest practice makes it possible to deal with problems. A pastor can talk to real people, but communication with an unnamed "they" remains elusive if not impossible.

Healthy staff relationships help close the back door of the church. They build unity, loyalty, and effectiveness. The result is a more attractive church to the people who attend. The magnetism of the fellowship holds the present members tight while attracting new ones. The quality of programming in every part of the church's activities shows improvement. The variety of needs that the chuch can meet continues to increase, but the need for added effectiveness will never cease.

GROWTH RATIOS VERSUS GROWTH-RESTRICTING
OBSTACLES

An effective multiple staff will enable a growing
church to keep growing. They will identify each
growth-restricting obstacle and set themselves to the
task of removing it. They will concentrate on breaking
the grip of sociological strangulation. Every church
leader and staff member is helped by knowing the
points where strangulation occurs. For centuries capable leaders have moved by intuition or a sixth sense.
Today careful research makes it possible to suggest
workable church-growth ratios. They provide a rule-of-
thumb guide as to when strangulation will restrict further growth.

A few leaders will object that a ratio leaves God's
leading out of the picture, but many honest Christian
thinkers find no incompatibility between God's supernatural working and his people's best efforts. The Holy
Spirit's direction and careful research into how
churches grow or decline are two sides of the same
coin. Both are necessary for maximum harvest. Research into patterns of growth or decline is developing
into a science. Books, doctoral dissertations, and data
compilations emerging from the church-growth movement provide valuable guidelines. Consider five
"growth ratios" that operate in harmony with one another. A couple of other growth-restricting obstacles
deserve consideration as well.

The first and most important ratio pertains to paid
staff. As given in chapter 3, the formula is (1+1):200. It

means one minister plus one secretary for every 200 people in average attendance. Growth will almost stop by the time the ratio reaches fulfillment. If a church is near the full ratio in either morning worship or Sunday School, *it needs to hire a new staff person.* In most churches the number of unpaid volunteers will not keep increasing without adding paid staff. Only as the number of lay leaders expands can the church keep growing.

The second ratio, 1:10, relates to the number of Sunday school classes meeting each week. For each pastor and each full-time person on the staff, including secretaries, the growing church will provide at least ten Sunday school classes. The 1:10 ratio counts only classes that meet on Sunday mornings. It assumes other cells will meet Sunday evening or during the week. The classes serve only as an index of the church's program, not its sum total of cells. A few growing churches accomplish the Christian education task through means other than Sunday school. They will adjust the ratio accordingly until it fits their situation.

If a church hires a staff member, but does not add Sunday school classes and other congregations and cells, growth will not happen. Too few places of welcome will be available. Closure will set in, and the back-door problem will become intense. On the other hand, if a church tries to add too many classes without adequate staffing, poor quality and low-morale problems will follow. The teacher turnover rate will run high because of a lack of support and encouragement. Numerous teachers will feel they either are not needed or are not doing an adequate job. For maximum results, the secret is the proper balance of all the ratios.

The third ratio governs the number of teachers needed for various ages of students. For children, the easy-to-remember guide is one teacher to the number of the age of the child. For example, six-year-olds follow a 1:6 ratio one teacher for six children. With seven-year-olds, the ratio becomes 1:7. In all of junior high, the ratio is 1:12. In high school it increases to 1:15. The appendix provides a more specific and detailed chart.[3]

For adults the class size depends on the teaching style. A discussion class will experience closure as it nears fifteen or twenty in attendance. The reason is that several members can no longer participate in the discussion. The attendance in a class specializing in learning activities will often level off between thirty-five and forty. A lecture class depends on the ability of the teacher to communicate effectively. Excellent lecturers can hold several hundred spellbound. Nevertheless, each lecture class will reach a point where attendance will level off.

Although a few exceptions can be found, the average class attendance throughout the Sunday school tends to approach the ratios listed in the appendix. Good growth-strategy calls for added teachers and smaller classes to begin the school year. On promotion day it makes sense to launch the new classes well below the expected average attendance per teacher. Then each teacher can strive for a reasonable growth goal to attain by Easter. The ratios suggested here will serve as helpful guidelines in goal setting. For example, just calculate what a healthy boost in attendance an increase of three students per class would give your Sunday school.

Enlarged Sunday school attendance, in turn, leads to additions in church membership.

An extraordinary teacher with a winsome personality can make an exception to the ratios; yet the rule-of-thumb guidelines prove true for the majority of teachers. What sometimes happens is that the fine work of an exceptional teacher is lost within a year. A large class moves forward into a new grade on promotion day in a single unit. Then under a more ordinary teacher attendance in the class begins to taper off until it nears the expected ratio. Smart leaders will observe the pattern and take corrective measures. They will divide the large class into two smaller groups with separate teachers, each with growing room.

The fourth ratio, the "75 percent rule" relates to space usage. What is deceptive about normal space use is how soon strangulation occurs. When a church reaches a year-round average worship attendance of 75 percent of its easy seating capacity, the growth rate will slow almost to a halt.[5] For short periods, or with high morale, a church can average more in worship attendance. Indeed, to average 75 percent with summer months and holidays included, most churches will seat people almost to capacity during the peak months. Without adding a new worship session or expanding the sanctuary or auditorium, however, the church will find it next to impossible to keep growing at its former rate.

More and more growing churches are offering multiple worship services or duplicate Sunday school sessions each Sunday morning. Experience shows that many people will worship at an hour other than 11:00 A.M. Sunday morning. Growing churches make the adjustment because their increasing attendance demands it. An early service added simply for convenience and not because of overcrowding will result in little, if any, growth, but multiple sessions often prove a great asset. The most successful patterns provide duplicate services at each hour; then neither worship session appears as second rate or in any way inferior to the other.

When adding Sunday school sessions, the best pattern is to schedule a class for every age at each hour. If worship runs simultaneously, families have the option of worshiping together and then studying during the other hours. The opposite pattern sometimes produces disastrous results. I refer to scheduling part of the family in worship and the rest in Sunday school during the same hour. Offering Sunday school for youth during one session and for children during the other with simultaneous worship both hours prevents many families from worshiping together. A few churches make the divided-family pattern work, but many flounder. Wise church leaders will investigate several successful patterns before making a change.

The fifth ratio concerns the square footage per person needed for maximum learning in Christian education. The needs vary with the age of the learner and the methods employed. The following recommendations allow room for each person to participate in activities such as group discussions and handwork. Obviously, a child sitting in a chair and listening passively requires a minimum amount of space, but for ideal participation the following ratios seem preferable. If overcrowding is a problem in your Sunday school, consider adding more workers or helpers to a class. Adding more teachers to a classroom will increase the number of students who can enjoy Sunday school and maximize learning (see the appendix, p. 143).

The youngest children, ages one to five, need the most space per person. God made them to wiggle and move, not to sit still. Their learning process includes exploring, touching, and playing as well as hearing. The recommended ratio for the tiny tots is 1:35, 1 child to 35 square feet of floor space. A department of 25 students, for example, would require 865 square feet of floor space. To calculate the ratio, measure all the square footage in a room, including the tables, cabinets, and other furniture using up space. A room 25 by 35 feet will accommodate 25 little ones well.

Elementary-age children need only slightly less space. The ratio is 1:25, 1 child to 25 square feet in the room. Space for displays, tables, chairs, easels, and storage is included. Elementary children need activities for effective learning too; yet their increased ability to accept organization allows them to function well in less space. The same size room mentioned above, 25 by 35 feet, will accommodate 10 more elementary children than preschoolers. When a department exceeds 35 or 40, division into two departments is often wise.

For youth and adults the ideal space ratio is 1:15. Each person can use 15 square feet of floor space. With adults, however, the space requirements vary with the teaching style. For example, a circle of chairs lends itself to discussion; rows of chairs suffice for a lecture. A room that allows 20 chairs in a circle may accommodate 40 chairs in rows. Any planning for future adult Christian education buildings must take into account the various teaching styles. The most versatile style is a large, open room with closing partitions that make it into smaller sections as needed.[6]

Sunday School classes of all ages too often restrict their growth by inefficient use of the available space. A sizable room may have one table with ten chairs around it. When more students arrive, the teacher crowds an extra chair or two around the table. Then the psychological factor of closure sets in, and the absentee rate increases. A second table and chairs, with the teacher standing between, would double the space usage. Some churches use department rooms during the first half of the hour and smaller classrooms during the second half. Placing some dividers in the large department rooms enables several more classes to meet.

Each class needs to feel full enough for good morale, but not too full lest complacency set in. Without fully realizing why, people feel uncomfortable in an over-crowded or empty classroom. Why not harness this psychological factor to add motivation for growth? It is amazing what 25 percent empty chairs will do to the desires of a class. With a fourth of the chairs empty, the members will muse to themselves, "We need some more people in here"; yet a room three-quarters full feels comfortable enough for effective teaching. Sunday school department leaders will do well to keep their eye on the seating capacity, striving for the "one-fourth empty chairs" balance.

The valid need for usable space drives many growing churches into a building program. The mention of buildings evokes accusations of the "edifice complex." Although it is easy to find churches whose declining attendance left them with half-empty facilities, it is next to impossible to find the opposite. Where are the growing, dynamic churches without buildings? They simply do not exist in highly specialized societies like our own. All the criticism of the edifice complex cannot eliminate the need for a church's own buildings. Growing churches need not feel guilt for building attractive and functional facilities essential for an expanding ministry.

Even with adequate buildings, too many churches choke their growth through limited parking facilities. The committed members of the church will walk an extra block or two and never complain. In a society conditioned by huge shopping centers with excess parking, however, the newcomers will be disturbed by parking problems. They may already feel uneasy because of their unfamiliarity with the worship style and anxious about meeting a new group of people. Not finding a convenient place to park may be the one excuse they need not to return. A count of empty parking spaces during the peak time on Sunday morning will reveal how many newcomers are still welcome.

A final growth-restricting obstacle, one that plagues hundreds of churches, is a sizable gap between age groups. Most growing churches either maintain a balance of all ages in the church or specialize in one age group. The first step in spotting such a gap is to check the attendance records. A simple bar graph showing the number of people in various age categories will help visualize the problem. Count the number of adults in their twenties, thirties, forties, fifties, and so on. What may stand out in visual perspective is a wide-open back door. People wanting fellowship with other families with similar age children or other adults with the same interests find their opportunities limited severely.

While measuring balance in age groupings, another study will also prove helpful. Make similar graphs for the opinion-makers in the church. What is the age balance among those who make the decisions about the future direction of the church? Although experience comes with age, God also places people of discernment in every age bracket. One more graph will shed new light. It will measure the age of volunteer workers of all kinds in the church. Enthusiastic volunteers constitute the best resource for more laborers. Therefore they must represent all age groups in order to keep in touch with every potential worker.

A careful analysis of each growth ratio and every known obstacle will reveal strangulation points. At least once a year church leaders will do well to "take inventory." With the hard facts in hand, their attention can turn to developing bold plans of faith. The pastor, staff, and lay leaders can begin to remove growth-restricting obstacles and implement growth-producing ideas. It is important to emphasize that thwarting of growth, not causes of numerical increase, is in view. No one factor alone accounts for all the variables. Church growth is far more complex than a simple ratio or a combination of ratios.

A rapid review of the highlights of the chapter will show what it takes to close the back door at least halfway. Recall some of the principal insights. Develop a worship celebration permeated by the Spirit of Christ. It offers a joyous experience with magnetic attraction to the person tempted to quit. Add congregations and multiply cells to expand the structure of the church;

then it will retain more members and serve them better. Nurture warm and loyal staff relationships that will build high morale and effective ministry. Implement church-growth ratios to prevent the possibility of "closure."

If ignored, any sociological factor can stop the church's growth! As hindrances to the grace of God, growth-restricting obstacles must go! Closing the back door, however, will accomplish little if only a few enter the front door, and an ongoing front-door effort will prove fruitful only if it focuses on people who will respond. To increase people-flow into the church, concentrate energy and resources on those most likely to be won. An understanding of *receptivity* and *homogeneous units* will enable a better appraisal of your church's sphere of influence. Along with a firm grasp of these principles the next chapter will give some guidelines for finding those who are responsive.

NOTES

1. C. Peter Wagner, *Your Church Can Grow* (Glendale, Cal.: Regal Books, 1976), pp. 97–109.
2. Richard A. Myers, *Program Expansion the Key to Church Growth* (Indianapolis, Ind.: Religious Research Center, 1970), pp. 5–6.
3. Richard A. Myers, *Factors That Affect Church School Class Size* (privately printed brochure, 1969), p. 7.
4. Lowell E. Brown, with Bobbie Reed, *Grow: Your Sunday School Can Grow* (Glendale, Cal.: Regal Books, 1974), pp. 53–57. Brown's ratios, while somewhat lower, tend to confirm Myers's research.
5. Medford Jones, *Let the Church Grow!* (South Bend, Ind.: Evangelical Church Building Corporation, 1968), p. 6.
6. For all space ratios, see Brown, *Grow,* pp. 76–77.

5. Focus on Your Evangelistic Bull's-Eye

"Church growth in receptive populations is marked by particularity."
—DONALD A. McGAVRAN

God brings families, communities, and even whole nations into brief periods of great receptivity to the gospel; yet all the harvest fields do not ripen at the same time. One community will show much responsiveness to the Christian message while another will appear resistant. Then again a resistant part of the population will turn receptive briefly. Receptivity fluctuates. In a time when more people will say yes to the gospel, the Lord of the harvest expects action. Under receptive conditions God desires his servants to gather large numbers of people to himself in a multitude of churches.

Gunnar Kjaerland, a missionary friend of mine from Norway, reported an obvious example. In sixty years the Norwegian Lutherans built a cluster of churches in mainland China that together had 4,000 members. Forced to move after the Communist takeover in 1949, their mission was transferred to Ethiopia. During the next twenty years the new Ethiopian churches took in

42,000 members. They experienced ten times as much growth as their sister denomination in mainland China in only one-third of the time; yet the same missionaries were using similar methods. What made the difference was a greater degree of receptivity.

Responsiveness will fluctuate because of a variety of circumstances. Most experienced pastors can testify to the differing receptivity at various times and places. What proved productive in one church reaped a small harvest in another. Pastors and church leaders with long tenure in one place can witness to a similar phenomenon. With the same philosophy of ministry far more people receive Christ at some periods than at others. Sometimes membership transfers from one church to another give a false sense of responsiveness, but discerning church leaders will note when more adults receive Christ for the first time than ever before. Transfers do not explain the marked change. The variableness in receptivity makes the difference.

IDENTIFYING RECEPTIVE PEOPLE

Pockets of responsiveness lie undiscovered in almost every community. How can pastors and church leaders find the most receptive non-Christians within their reach? What does a person look for to spot responsiveness? First, wherever some churches are growing through conversions from the world receptivity exists. The best sign of an openness to a change for Christ in your community is the growth of a few nearby churches. Pastors and church leaders find it a grave temptation to rationalize when other churches grow and theirs do not, but excuses will not change the facts. Conversion growth can happen only where people are receptive to the gospel.

The receptivity of the unchurched to the gospel of Christ is on the increase in the United States today. In almost every corner of the land a few churches are logging impressive growth rates. In rural areas, small towns, and suburbs some churches are expanding. Surprising new church growth is happening among the dozens of ethnic groups for whom English is a second language. The current receptivity in the United States may not last long. Harvest time never does. For the present, however, responsiveness is moving toward the receptive side of the scale. A growing church is an exciting experience for many and a live option for many more. *Where some churches are growing, others can.*

Second, receptivity appears wherever people are "in transition." Those who make a major change in life—residence, occupation, marriage, first baby, for example—are often open to new ideas. Many will want to commit their lives to Jesus Christ. As the ministry of your church touches their lives, some will become responsible members. A study from the Synod of Texas, "Why People Join the Presbyterian Church, U.S.," documents this type of receptivity.

> Virtually all the new members, in describing the circumstances under which they first began thinking of joining, talk about circumstances that involve some major change in their personal situation—marriage, geographical move, vocational change, illness, death, birth of children, going away from home to college or service.[1]

Third, God is preparing hearts for the gospel wherever people are "under tension." Every pastor knows that human extremity is God's opportunity. People who are hurting reach for what they really believe in the depths of their soul. God, prayer, and the good news of Christ come alive in a new way. Tensions from family frustrations, economic pressures, and personal crises prepare people for a new encounter with Christ. As an alert church leader you will see people under tension as persons needing both humanitarian service and the life-changing gospel of our Lord Jesus Christ. You will not want to miss the opportunity for witness in word and deed.

A word of caution seems necessary here. People who are making a major change and people who are hurting remain open to the wrong kinds of influence as well as to the right ones. False religions, materialistic substitutes, and easy answers from "pop" psychology may hold an unusual appeal. People open to change stand at a crossroads. The Christian messenger urges them to take the narrow way to life, but a thousand other voices urge them to take the easy road to destruction. Receptivity by itself will in no way guarantee the growth of your church. It only provides the responsiveness by which your congregation can win those who are open if it will.

DETERMINING EVANGELISTIC PRIORITIES

The lesson for growing churches is to develop strategic priorities in evangelism. Every church must face up to the reality of limited resources. No church has unlim-

ited time, money, energy, and human leadership. Since
you cannot do everything, you must do the best things.
Wise leaders will concentrate their evangelistic resources on the winnable. If you can fish from any hole
in a stream, why not go where the trout are biting? You
may not land every fish that nibbles, but your chance
of catching your limit is far better than if none are
biting. Concentrating on those who like the style, personality, and programs of your church is good strategy.

To set your evangelistic priorities straight, ask, Which
of the receptive will be attracted by our kind of church?
Compare the receptive people to the circles of a target.
The bull's-eye are first-time visitors to worship or any
Christian activity who profess no personal relationship
to Jesus Christ. Some accepted an invitation to church
or a Christian activity precisely because they were "in
transition" or "under tension." Their attendance shows
that God grabbed their attention for a fleeting moment.
If you want church growth, you will focus on your
evangelistic bull's-eye—the winnable among first-time
visitors.

The secret is to build redemptive friendships immediately. In any of a dozen ways, the growing church
will communicate the gospel to visitors. Some do it at
once with a return visit to the newcomer's home. Others take time for friendship building first. If exercised,
the lost art of Christian hospitality can touch many a
newcomer for the Lord. Next to an open heart, an open
home is one of the most wonderful attractions. The
Christian home radiates the love, joy, and peace of
Christ without pretending to be perfect. Instinctively
the newcomer feels welcome and senses the warm ap-

peal of Christ's love. Whatever your way of communicating love and the life-changing gospel of Christ, you must not neglect these opportunities.

The inner circle of your evangelistic target, the one just around the bull's-eye, stands for the responsive among your "near neighbors." Dozens of people who might turn their lives over to Christ live close to your church or the homes of your members. They may feel comfortable with your church members in settings such as school, work, or social functions, but they never darken the door of the church nor show up at anything labeled "Christian." Their economic and educational situations are similar enough to present no social barrier. They live nearby not only in geography but also in many matters of taste, preference, and style. When it comes to faith, values, morals, and meaning, however, these near neighbors do not consciously follow Jesus Christ; yet many of them are winnable.

As informed leaders know, the church building only houses the people of God for worship, education, and fellowship. The church itself is found wherever God's people live and move. The members of your church have "near neighbors" where they work, go to school, and spend their leisure time. For maximum growth you will want to help your members recruit, evangelize, and disciple near neighbors wherever they may be found. Because of the recent emphasis on witnessing, many are aware of speaking up for Christ. They already sense that people who are hurting are often ready to respond. In addition, you will teach them to concentrate on people making a major change. Simple kindness shown to newcomers in the neighborhood, at

work, or at school can build friendships as a bridge for
the gospel.

The next circle of the target represents the "near
neighbors" who live within reasonable travel time of
the church buildings. Twelve miles distance or fifteen
to twenty minutes driving time is a workable guideline
for reasonable travel. A few churches use radio or tele-
vision to touch a broader community. Many more use
newspaper stories, pictures, and paid advertising to
give their church greater exposure. Most churches,
however, receive only limited response from advertising. Without a personal recommendation few non-
Christians will attend a church for the first time; yet
energetic leaders know that advertising and newspaper
coverage build an awareness of their church. Then as
recruiters issue personal invitations, more people accept.

For your local church, one of the outer rings of the
target represents people of a differing "homogeneous
unit." These people live at a great distance in terms of
language, culture, or socioeconomic level. In church-
growth jargon each of these groups is a "homogeneous
unit." Donald A. McGavran, recognized leader of the
church growth movement, explains homogeneous
units in simple terms. "The *homogeneous unit* is simply
a section of society in which all members have some
characteristic in common."[2] The most obvious characteristic is language.[2] Closely associated are cultural and
ethnic qualities. Within these more obvious boundaries
are lesser distinguishing marks such as socioeconomic
similarities and preferences in style and taste.

A striking distinction between one homogeneous
unit and another is "people consciousness." A sure sign

of the existence of people consciousness is a "we" usage in the vocabulary as opposed to "they." Returning to the target analogy, "they" may live close to your church as measured by mileage or minutes, but "they" live at a great distance in people consciousness. The chasm appears in life-style, in values, and especially in the forms of heart-to-heart communication. Overtones of people consciousness enter into every style of communication and form of worship. Thus, what attracts one person to a certain church will repel another. The same principle applies to evangelistic potency. Your kind of church may win a few of another homogeneous unit to Christ and to responsible membership, but do not expect a sudden influx of their relatives and friends. The unconverted peers will feel little heart attraction to your kind of church.

A few churches solve the we-they problem by developing several congregations within their structure, each suited to a particular homogeneous unit. Temple Baptist Church in the heart of Los Angeles houses Korean, Hispanic, Chinese, and English-speaking congregations. Once each three months they join together in a Sounds of Heaven service. The massed congregation sings the same hymn in several languages simultaneously. The four pastors read biblical affirmations in sequence, and the congregation responds with "Hallelujah" or "Hosanna" in their several languages. On most Sundays the congregations worship separately in various parts of the sprawling facility that once housed six thousand. Their multicongregation, multilanguage approach fits the demographic complexion of the inner city.[4]

Multiple congregations with simultaneous worship

services require a large facility, but some smaller
churches are opening their building at a different hour
for worship in other languages. They are making an
intensive effort to launch new congregations among
differing homogeneous units. Ralph E. Longshore, a
Southern Baptist minister in California, reports that the
Southern Baptists in the state of California now preach
the gospel in twenty-nine languages each week. Some
of these meet in the church buildings of English-speaking Southern Baptist congregations. Other mission
churches meet in a home, rented facility, or their own
building. Either way, the basic idea of starting a new
church that fits the people consciousness of the neighborhood seems to be catching on.

Churches in communities making a drastic change in
ethnic makeup face a difficult task. No one model will
meet the variety of needs. Often attempts to integrate
differing homogeneous units have led to stagnation and
decline in membership. Many churches fail to see the
multiple-congregation model. Others feel a great dis-
comfort in changing their worship style and programming. The preferences of residents with a differing people-consciousness do not match their own. Still others
do not know what change to make, nor do they have
the ability to do it even if they so desired. When the
congregation wants to relocate, tension arises; yet for
many churches relocation may be the only way to sur-
vive.

Instead of opposing relocation in every instance,
try a new strategy. Returned missionaries or denominational specialists may help launch a new congregation that fits the community. The congregation con-

sidering relocation sometimes can also take a giant step of faith by refusing to sell its old facility. It was built in the community by the tithes and offerings of people living there. It can continue as an ongoing witness to Jesus Christ there. The ideal transition is to a new congregation of the same denomination. Where such a step is impossible, a sale to a church of similar beliefs is the next best choice. In either case, denominational financial assistance can help make the transition possible.

CULTURE AND HOMOGENEOUS UNITS

All the talk about homogeneous units sticks in the craw of many church leaders. The subject often becomes an emotional issue generating more heat than light. Church-growth researchers know that people in great numbers seldom become Christian outside their own homogeneous unit.[5] Applying the homogeneous unit principle to evangelism with discernment and the Holy Spirit's direction results in greater growth. More people find Christ, more individuals continue in a life of discipleship, more congregations thrive, and more new churches begin. Some critics reply that practical results do not guarantee the rightness of the homogeneous unit concept; so the discerning Christian will want answers from the Scriptures. I believe the homogeneous unit principle does *not* violate God's Word.

Culture itself is God-given. Culture or people-consciousness is the bottom line in distinguishing a homogeneous unit. It is but another way of describing the biblical concept of *ethnos,* usually translated "nation" or "people." I place culture in the category of "creation order." Since every society has marriage and government in some form, theologians speak of them as creation orders. Because marriage and government contribute to the betterment of life, theologians figure that these creation orders come from God's hand. I consider culture a part of God's governing hand over the peoples of the earth, a subdivision of the "government" creation order. It compares to the family being God's institution because it is part of the "marriage" creation order.

The creation orders contain a flaw however. Human sinfulness warps every part of existence. Sin leads to bad marriages, broken homes, corrupt governments, and pagan cultures. Rebellion and brokenness bring discord and heartache into all social relationships, even those created by God himself. Like human nature, culture reflects both God's creative hand and the damage of sin. Because of sin, every culture has points of conflict with the gospel, but the very brokenness also means every culture stands in need of the healing touch of Jesus Christ.

No Christian has the right to abolish one of God's creation orders. One can speak with a prophetic voice about specific wrongs in the government, but government as a function remains good and necessary. It is wrong to call for anarchy. A concerned Christian can criticize bad marriages, but calling for the abolition of marriage itself is contrary to Scripture. In the same way Christians can speak out against abuses and distortions within cultures, but they dare not call for the abolition of a culture itself. Indeed, because each culture is part of God's creation order, it will contain practices and values compatible with Christ's teaching. The wise strategy for discerning Christians is to affirm the strengths of a given culture and work to change its weaknesses.

Church history teaches us not to pursue the elusive dream of a fully Christian culture. It is simple bigotry to assume any one culture is so Christian that all others must conform to it. Nor can the company of the committed expect any success by withdrawing from the corrupt cultures around them. All attempts to create a Christian culture pure and untarnished by the outside world have led to failure. The only pattern that produced remarkable results in the past was the one recommended by Jesus. Christians served as witnesses, salt and light *in* the world, while maintaining primary loyalty to Christ's kingdom. To the extent that they were obedient to their divine calling, their influence "Christianized" their cultures, improving and lifting them.

As each culture feels the influence of Christ's people, it begins to reflect something of the glory of God. Each cultural expression of true worship, for example, lends its own beauty to the adoration of God. In decision-making processes each homogeneous church reveals new insights into how God leads his people. Like a diamond reflecting light, each Christianized culture gives fresh insights into the wonder of God's own nature. Christian unity does not mean crushing cultural diversity. The unity among Christians of various cultural backgrounds develops in their love for the one

Lord and Savior, Jesus Christ. Lasting unity, however, will not emerge automatically, but only by mutual submission to the authority of God's Word and Spirit.

We must note here the all-important distinction between culture and color. They are not the same. A church may be fully integrated as far as color is concerned, and yet represent only one culture. In fact, a basic misunderstanding of the homogeneous-unit principle lies precisely at this point. Too many people see only racial overtones in the term "homogeneous units." Such a distortion is the last thing intended by church-growth leaders. Like the conscientious among God's people everywhere, they feel chagrined at any report of one racial group excluding another. Students of the church-growth movement know that its leaders denounce racial prejudice as intolerable sin.[6] My strong conviction is that any Christian church that excludes members of any other racial group brings disgrace to the name of Christ.

Following the homogeneous unit principle also adds evangelistic potency. Research of the growth of churches worldwide substantiates a fundamental axiom. As McGavran states it, "Men like to become Christian in their own social groupings, without crossing barriers." Hardly anywhere in the world are heterogeneous churches growing by conversions to Christ; yet the examples of homogeneous churches with evangelistic effectiveness are too numerous to count. The overwhelming evidence is that God honors the homogeneous-unit principle in fulfilling the Great Commission.

ARE HOMOGENEOUS CHURCHES REALLY CHRISTIAN?

When McGavran speaks of people becoming Christian "without crossing barriers," the obstacles he has in mind are social, not theological.[7] Only genuine repentance can move barriers of sin that stand in the way of becoming Christian. Personal faith in Jesus Christ is God's call, not up for compromise. The stumbling block of the cross, the invitation to turn from sin, the requirement to give first place to Christ as Lord of life, all remain irreplaceable, but social barriers must go. All people need a church where they can worship in their native tongue. All Christians desire to worship God in ways they find meaningful and deeply expressive among their own people. All nonbiblical barriers to becoming a genuine Christian and responsible member of Christ's church must be torn down.

No one questions the existence of homogeneous churches, each with its own style of worship and pattern of government. The vast majority of churches, and almost all the growing ones, are in fact homogeneous. The question posed by some critics is whether they ought to exist. Do not homogeneous churches cause divisiveness in the body of Christ? they ask. Do they not reinforce racial prejudice? Do they not deny the unity of Christ's body? Do they not permit a kind of apartheid in the Christian fellowship?[9]

If homogeneous churches in reality are not Christian, then radical changes must take place at once. Leaders must throw to the wind the warning from growth spokesmen that forcing a church to become hetero-

geneous leads to its decline and decay. They must insist
on mixing homogeneous units and crushing cultural
diversity. On the other hand, if homogeneous churches
are really Christian, then the persistent questions asked
by the critics will serve as warning signals. Anything
God-given faces the possibility of distortion. Leaders of
homogeneous churches must work to build unity
among all Christians. Like a soldier on sentinel duty,
thcy will watch for the danger of reinforcing prejudice
or sanctioning other sins. A key question is relevant to
the church today and holds vital importance for its future.

Are homogeneous churches really Christian? My answer is "yes, if . . ." and "not unless. . . ." *Yes, if* their
doors and their hearts remain open to members of
other homogeneous units who want to hear the gospel,
receive Christ, and join their church. *Not unless* their
attitudes as well as their actions reveal ". . . you are all
one in Christ Jesus" (Galatians 3:28). No Christian
church has the right to withhold the gospel from anyone who desires it. Nor does it have the right to deny
admittance to church membership or to any level of
leadership within the congregation on racial grounds.
To do so is less than fully Christian. With open hearts
and open doors, homogeneous churches are really
Christian.

Scripture itself gives a legitimate basis for homogeneous units. Beginning with God's covenant with
Abraham (see Genesis 12:1–3) the people of Israel were
chosen as a distinctive homogeneous unit. Old Testament Israel forms the most distinct homogeneous
group in the Bible. The Lord even required ethnic

separation (see Genesis 24:1–4; 28:1–5). His purpose was to develop the new people through whom he could work out his redemptive purpose. Gentiles from other homogeneous groups did join the covenant people of God from time to time, but to do so, they had to leave their own cultural people and cross the social barriers to join Israel.

In order to count themselves among God's people, Gentile converts faced up to a double demand. They had no choice but to become Hebrews both in culture and in religion. One could cite exceptions such as Melchizedek (see Genesis 14:18–20) and Balaam (see Numbers 22–24) who had direct communication with God without joining the covenant community, but their relationship to him and his people remains vague. The Old Testament revealed clearly only one way for people to relate themselves to the Lord God. It called for joining themselves to Israel, including the rite of circumcision. In other words, they had to forsake their own cultural roots and bind their life-style to one distinctive homogeneous unit, Israel.

By New Testament times Israel had homogeneous groups within itself. The Jews of Jesus' day recognized three social groupings—Judeans, Galileans, and Hellenists. The differences were more than geographical. The Judeans spoke Aramaic and considered themselves the authentic expression of Israel. As religious purists, their leaders insisted on scrupulous observance of the Law of Moses and the traditions of the fathers. Politically, they cooperated with Rome, the Gentile occupation forces who ruled the Holy Land. The Galileans spoke Aramaic with a different accent than the Judeans

(see Matthew 26:73). They were somewhat less conscientious about the intricacies of tradition. Consequently,
they felt the sting of disdain from the Judeans who
considered them inferior. Politically, the Galileans
were ardent patriots, itching to throw off Roman rule.

Even greater cultural differences were evident with
the Hellenists, Jews dispersed among the major cities of
the Roman world. They spoke Greek as their first language (see Acts 6:1) and even had their own synagogues
in Jerusalem (see Acts 6:9).[11] Many had lived in Gentile
surroundings all their lives, tracing their roots back to
the devastation of the Northern Kingdom of Israel in
722 B.C. or the Southern Kingdom of Judah in 586 B.C.
Since they were tinged with the contamination of Gentile culture, the Judeans especially took a dim view of
their life-style;[12] yet in politics, they accepted Roman
rule as a fact of life much as the Judeans did. A few of
the Hellenists, like Saul of Tarsus, prided themselves on
Roman citizenship.

The three homogeneous groupings—Judeans, Galileans, and Hellenists—were noticeable within Israel;
yet a far deeper division among men in the first century
existed between Jews and Gentiles.[13] Over the centuries both groups built high walls of prejudice. Racial,
cultural, and especially religious barriers separated
them (Ephesians 2:14). From one perspective, the Jews
had everything religiously: "the adoption as sons and
the glory and the covenants and the giving of the Law
and the temple service and the promises, whose are the
fathers, and from whom is the Christ according to the
flesh" (Romans 9:4–5). From this perspective, the Gentiles had nothing. They were ". . . separate from Christ,

excluded from the commonwealth of Israel, and strangers to the covenants of promise, having no hope and without God in the world" (Ephesians 2:12).

Many Jews avoided intimate social contact with Gentiles unless they became "God-fearers" who joined in synagogue worship (see Acts 13:16, 43); yet among Jews who followed Jesus as Messiah something new was happening. Because of the reconciling atonement of Jesus Christ on the cross, Gentiles did not find themselves excluded from the church. Gentiles who trusted Christ gained equal footing with believing Jews regardless of racial or cultural differences (see Ephesians 2:11–22). No longer were they second-class citizens, but rather an essential part of Christ's church. What is fascinating is that they became part of the true Israel of God without becoming culturally Jewish first. This has important implications for the issues of evangelism and homogeneous units today.

A NEW TESTAMENT BASIS FOR HOMOGENEOUS UNITS

With deep Jewish roots, the earliest Jerusalem believers quite naturally expected all Gentiles who joined their ranks to become Jewish proselytes. In other words, they felt that all disciples of Jesus must belong to one cultural homogeneous unit. Why should they not expect circumcision, abstinence from certain food, and mandatory temple worship from Gentile Christians? Neither their new identity as the true people of God nor their commission to take the gospel to enlighten the Gentiles did anything to undermine their scruples on such issues. God, however, revealed to Paul that

Gentiles could become full disciples without circumcision and the legal intricacies of the ceremonial law. The revelation proved revolutionary in making Gentile converts to Christ. It meant they were to become fully Christian within their own homogeneous units, without crossing social barriers.

So dramatic was the breakthrough that Paul spoke of his apostolic ministry and evangelistic church planting among the Gentiles as ". . . the gospel of uncircumcision" (Galatians 2:7, literal translation as noted in NASB margin). The term "gospel of uncircumcision" meant God commissioned Paul to preach to the Gentiles, just as Peter was to preach the "gospel of circumcision" to the Jews, but it involved much more. The circumcision-uncircumcision controversy in New Testament times included theological and cultural issues as well. No wonder it was one of the most divisive issues facing the church. Paul saw clearly that the integrity of the gospel was at stake. He taught that the true circumcision was an inward attitude of the heart (see Romans 2:25–29, Philippians 3:3).

For a Gentile Christian who trusted Jesus Christ as Lord and Savior, physical circumcision was a matter of indifference. What really mattered was the faith, love, and obedience of the new person in Christ. Otherwise circumcision became just one more work of the law. It amounted to nothing more than a futile attempt to achieve righteousness before God while bypassing faith in Jesus Christ. Nor did circumcision add anything of spiritual value to a person already justified by faith. His progress toward Christian maturity was in no way helped by such legalistic means. In summary, circumcision presented an obstacle in understanding the true nature of the gospel as based on grace, not on one's works of the law.

The "gospel of uncircumcision" also held important cultural implications. Christian Gentiles did not have to adhere to the Jewish dietary restrictions. They could freely ignore Jerusalem temple worship and Sabbath regulations. It meant freedom from restrictions that covered dress, diet, friendships, feasts, and festivals. Gentile converts to Jesus Christ did not cross the nearly insurmountable social and cultural obstacles to become Jewish in life style. In short, they did not change homogeneous units. Of course, any person savingly regenerated by Christ made a moral change (see Ephesians 4:17–5:20), but in tastes, preferences, styles, likes, and dislikes both Jew and Gentile believers could remain in their distinctive homogenous groups.

Did the local churches in New Testament times worship in homogeneous units? No one knows for certain, but the house-church pattern almost guarantees that at times they did. It is a grave misunderstanding to imagine only one congregation in each city named in the New Testament. Since church buildings did not exist in the earliest centuries of Christianity, on most Sundays congregations worshiped in private homes throughout the city. In Romans 16, for example, Paul sends greetings to five households, or "house-churches."[14] Because conversions to Christ most often followed household lines, the natural result was for a few families and friends to worship together. Often they were the very people who knew one another before turning to Christ. Worshiping in private homes with kinship and friend-

ship ties means they often developed the homogeneous
unit pattern.

In Christ both Jews and Gentiles became one,
forming the new humanity (see Ephesians 2:15). They
belonged to the one body of Christ and were ind-
welt by the one Spirit (see Ephesians 4:4). They
found unity in Christ, not in cultural conformity.
Jews were free to continue in all the traditions of the
ceremonial law and rituals of temple worship (see
Acts 21:17–26). Gentiles remained free to worship the
Lord without them. Salvation for both came from
faith in Christ and from him alone. The end result of
proclaiming the "gospel of uncircumcision" was that
Gentiles came to Christ without leaving their own
homogeneous units.[15]

Under the inspiration of the Holy Spirit, Paul
removed cultural stumbling blocks to the gospel; so
must church leaders today. The demand that every
local church mix various social, ethnic, and cultural
peoples into a single heterogeneous group presents
such an unnecessary stumbling block. Many non-Christians will reject the gospel if it means aligning themselves with a congregation outside their own homogeneous unit. Preconditions that require seeking
unbelievers to cross cultural and social barriers are dan-
gerous to the faith. Such requirements amount to deny-
ing the validity of the "gospel of uncircumcision" in the
Bible. If God had not favored the homogeneous unit
method of allowing people to become Christians without crossing cultural barriers, he would never have led
Paul to take a non-circumcision approach to the Gentiles.

CRITICISM OF THE HOMOGENEOUS UNIT PRINCIPLE

Critics who oppose the homogeneous unit approach to evangelism on theological grounds cite certain proof texts. Almost without exception they quote Paul, who stressed the oneness found in Christ (see 1 Corinthians 12:13, Galatians 3:28, Ephesians 2:11–22, Colossians 3:11). Paul, however, was the very apostle who preached the "gospel of uncircumcision" that included homogeneous unit evangelism. Since Paul would not contradict himself, what was he saying? I believe he was fighting on two fronts. On the one hand, he defended a non-circumcision approach to Gentile evangelism and church life. On the other hand, he opposed excluding anyone from the church on racial or cultural grounds. He taught that in Christ Jews and Gentiles are made "into one new man, thus establishing peace" (Ephesians 2:15).

Once a group of either Jews or Gentiles enters Christ's kingdom, it has no right to exclude anyone of another homogeneous unit. A person's social, racial, or cultural background makes no difference. If a person receives Jesus Christ as Lord and Savior, he also belongs to the same people of God. The doors of the church must remain open to all who will become disciples of Christ Jesus. Of course, the church is obligated to hold reasonable standards of membership that do not deny its Christian reputation; but once a person makes a credible profession of faith in Christ, he cannot be excluded from the church on the basis of race, color, or class. Nor can a person be barred from holding any office of leadership in the congregation because of racial origins, as some cultists teach. No exclusion is ever permitted.

Paul is *not* saying a person or group must lose its cultural identity in order to become truly Christian and a full member of the church. In my judgment scholars who declare that in Christ both Jews and Gentiles lose their cultural identity go beyond what the apostle intended.[16] A person's ethnic and cultural identity has a God-given quality. It is a fundamental part of one's personality. Paul's point is not the necessity of losing cultural, ethnic, or sexual identity. What he meant is that the new relationship with Christ denies any exclusion from the Christian fellowship. Even more profound, Christ provides a true unity deeper than any human barrier.

Where then does the body of Christ visibly demonstrate its unity before the watching world? The new Israel (see Galatians 6:16) is after all a new humanity (see Ephesians 2:11–16) that heals social divisions. One effective way of showing unity is fellowship among various congregations. Any wholesome activity that shows cooperation with Christians from other homogeneous churches is desirable. Where can different styles and preferences operate with more validity than on the intercongregational level? In such a setting each congregation maintains its identity and retains its own personality. Its leadership style and power structure for decision making are not threatened; yet all belong to one another in Christ.

One of the church's crucial tasks in the next decade is to demonstrate the oneness of the body of Christ. Admittedly, most denominations need to work harder here; so do local churches in building bridges of fellowship to congregations of other homogeneous units. The wise church will get outside itself and outside its own homogeneous fellowship on occasion. It will find opportunities to manifest openly its oneness in Christ with other homogeneous churches. It will also give itself to extending the gospel to other homogeneous units in cross cultural evangelism.

A primary point of this chapter is that becoming Christians within homogeneous units is the biblical pattern. The Bible teaches church leaders to hold two factors in balance. They must deny any exclusion on racial or social grounds, and they must also beware of any forced attempts to mix different homogeneous groups. The biblical balance is found somewhere between these two extremes. One important question for homogeneous churches is, Were people of other homogeneous units excluded, or did they prefer not to participate? Only if a church begins to exclude other races or social classes does it violate the biblical norm. Another vital question is, Is this homogeneous church seeking fellowship with Christians of different homogeneous units?

For evangelistic potency the effective church will focus on its receptive bull's-eye. It will concentrate prayer and personnel on the most receptive. It will train its people to remain alert as Christ's witnesses to people "in transition" and "under tension." Yet it will hold with an open hand all who accept Christ through its sharing of the gospel. It will allow those who are not comfortable with its style to find a Christ-centered congregation where they feel at home. With such a gracious spirit and open-handed policy, a church will find it becomes more homogeneous, not less. It follows that it will most readily attract people who prefer its style of worship, preaching, fellowship, and service. The end result is that its evangelistic potency increases and the church grows.

Leaders of growing churches believe God causes the growth, so they cooperate with his principles. What are these principles, these secrets for growing churches? In this book I have discussed the following: high morale, obedience to the Lord's mandates, mobilization of lay-persons as recruiters, evangelists, and disciplers, building an effective multiple staff, multiplying circles of commitment, and increasing evangelistic efforts toward the people most receptive to each kind of church. In addition, alert church leaders will attempt to remove growth-restricting obstacles by applying the proper ratios to staff, facilities, and services.

I believe in the church as the body of Christ. Local churches come to the rescue of those who hurt, give purpose for living from the Bible, and bring people into right relationship with the living Lord. Effective churches help people to become all God intended them to be. They get outside themselves to touch the world around them with God's love and message of salvation. In this receptive time many churches are growing, and others can!

NOTES

1. Charles M. Olsen, *The Base Church* (Atlanta, Ga.: Forum House Publishers, 1973), pp. 140–41.
2. Donald A. McGavran, *Understanding Church Growth* (Grand Rapids, Mich.: Wm. B. Eerdmans, 1970), p. 85.

3. For a discussion of homogeneous units in church-growth writings, see McGavran, *Understanding Church Growth,* pp. 85–87, 183–215, and C. Peter Wagner, *Your Church Can Grow,* a self-study pack (Department of Church Growth, Fuller Evangelistic Association, Box 989, Pasadena, Cal. 91102, 1976), pp. 22–27, and tapes 4 and 5.

4. Jim Townsend, "A Tourniquet for the Inner City," *Church Growth: America,* May–June 1976, pp. 1, 5.

5. McGavran, *Understanding Church Growth,* p. 191.

6. Ibid., pp. 208–12. Donald A. McGavran and Win C. Arn, *How to Grow a Church* (Glendale, Cal.: Regal Books, 1973), p. 46. Wagner, *Your Church Can Grow,* pp. 114–15.

7. McGavran and Arn, *How to Grow a Church,* p. 45.

8. McGavran, *Understanding Church Growth,* p. 191.

9. *The Pasadena Consultation,* a colloquium on the Homogeneous Unit Principle held May 31–June 2, 1977), p. 3, available in mimeographed form from *Church Growth: America* magazine, c/o Institute of American Church Growth, 150 S. Robles, Pasadena, Cal. 91101. Every person interested in the theological implications of the homogeneous unit principle should read this summary statement by the Lausanne Theology and Education Group.

10. G. Ernest Wright, ed., *Great People of the Bible and How They Lived* (Pleasantville, N.Y.: The Reader's Digest Association, Inc., 1974), pp. 336–43.

11. F. F. Bruce, *Commentary on the Book of Acts,* New International Commentary Series (Grand Rapids, Mich.: Wm. B. Eerdmans, 1956), p. 128.

12. G. Ernest Wright, ed., *Great People of the Bible and How They Lived,* pp. 385–86.

13. F. F. Bruce, *Commentary on the Epistle to the Colossians,* New International Commentary Series (Grand Rapids, Mich.: Wm. B. Eerdmans, 1957), p. 211.

14. F. F. Bruce, *The Epistle of Paul to the Romans: An Introduction and Commentary,* Tyndale Series (Grand Rapids, Mich.: Wm. B. Eerdmans, 1963), pp. 266–67.

15. For a scholarly treatment see Ernest DeWitt Burton, *A Critical and Exegetical Commentary on the Epistle to the Galatians,* International Critical Commentary Series (Edinburgh: T. & T. Clark, 1921), p. 92.

16. For an example, see Ralph P. Martin, *"Ephesians"* in *The Broadman Bible Commentary,* Vol. 2, ed. Clifton J. Allen (Nashville, Tenn.: Broadman Press, 1971), p. 144.

Appendix: Crucial Factors in Church Growth

1. COMPONENTS OF COMPOSITE CHURCH GROWTH
Rose Drive Friends Church, 1963–1978

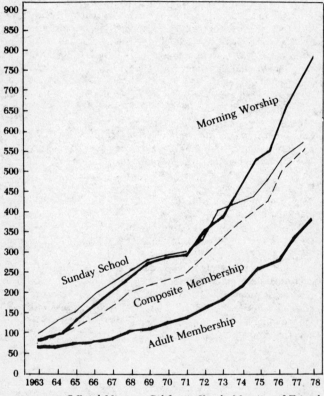

SOURCE: *Official Minutes,* California Yearly Meeting of Friends Church (Whittier, Ca.: 1979).

In a young church, attendance at morning worship and Sunday School is much greater than adult membership. In older congregations this would seldom be the case. Why not make a similar graph for your church? The purpose of figuring composite membership (the average of the other three) is to balance all three components and give a more accurate growth picture of any local church (see pages 41–43).

2. RELATIONSHIP OF CHURCH MEMBERSHIP TO NUMBER OF PAID STAFF

| Staff Requirements | | | | | Church Membership | | Number of Sunday School Classes | Sunday School Attendance |
Pastor	Associate Minister	Dir. or Min. of Ed.	Volunteer Secretary	Paid Secretary	Type I Members	Type II Members		
x					150	50	10	90
x			x		300	75	15	130
x				part-time	500	100	19	190
x				full-time	700	130	25	280
x		x		1 or 2	900	180	30	350
x	x	x		2 or 3	1,400	300	45	500
x	2	x		4 to 6	2,100	450	65	700

SOURCE: Richard A. Myers.

Membership and Sunday school attendance figures listed are the maximums that can be expected before growth will level off. This will vary somewhat from church to church, since different denominations hold different philosophies of church membership. Type I memberships include both active and inactive members. In general, Type I churches report the number of members related to the church in the recent past, whether or not those members have a current meaningful relationship with the congregation. Type II memberships include only the number of active adult members currently participating in a church's program. In general, Type II churches do not report the constituents who participate but have never formally joined the church.

3. RELATIONSHIP OF SUNDAY SCHOOL CLASS MEMBERSHIP TO NUMBER OF TEACHERS

Number of Teachers per Class:	1	2	3
Departments	Number of Students per Class		
NURSERY			
2-year-olds	4	8	12
3-year-olds	4	8	12
KINDERGARTEN			
4-year-olds	5	10	15
5-year-olds	5	10	15
PRIMARY			
1st grade	6	10	15
2nd grade	7	12	16
3rd grade	7	12	16
JUNIOR			
4th grade	8	13	17
5th grade	8	13	17
6th grade	9	14	19
JUNIOR HIGH			
7th–8th grades together	10	16	21
7th grade	12	18	23
8th grade	12	18	23
SENIOR HIGH			
9th–12th grades together	12	18	23
or			
9th–10th grades together	12	18	23
11th–12th grades together	12	18	23
or			
9th grade	15	22	28
10th grade	15	22	28
11th grade	15	22	28
12th grade	15	22	28
ADULTS			
Lecture classes	40 or more		
Discussion classes	15–20		

SOURCE: Richard A. Myers, *Factors That Affect Church School Size* (Indianapolis: Religious Research Center, p. 7).

Team teaching by two or three teachers for each Sunday School class tends to increase membership at the rate shown here. But the alternative of adding *new* classes in each age group, each with its own teacher, will increase membership faster than the increase by team teaching, from the primary department to adults. For the faster growth by multiplying classes a church will need adequate space.

Index